Pagan Portals

Temple of the Bones

Rituals to the Goddess Hekate

What people are saying about

Hekate: Temple of the Bones

The relationship that Bird has with Hekate is palpable; rich and deep, with an undercurrent of ancient mystery. I have attended Several Temple of the Bones rituals, and Hekate's glittering presence shone through with great clarity and beauty in each one. Whether you've loved Hekate for many years, or seek to know her better now, you could not ask for a better guide than Bird.

Sharon Knight, Musician and Producer of Hexenfest

This book is a gift to the modern witchcraft community. Part spell book, part ritual grimoire, and part lived experience; this book offers guidance on how to approach working with an ancient Goddess. Hekate is formidable, and Teixeira doesn't shy away from the hard truths of working with Her. Recommended as a starting point for new witches and ritualists or as a reference for older practitioners.

Iris Meredith Bell, General Manager of The Raven's Wing Magical Co.

Temple of the Bones is the book I wished I'd had when I first met Hekate in my witchcraft journey. The language and practices are accessible, the magick palpable in each page. There is a deep concern and care for the reader, while also a reverence that invites attention and sincere devotion. I am grateful for this book and the way it welcomed me into the rituals.

Irisanya Moon, author of Reclaiming Witchcraft and Aphrodite

Temple of the Bones - Rituals to the Goddess Hekate by Jennifer Teixeira is a superb book of practical rites to honour the ancient

Goddess of the crossroads, keeper of the keys to mysteries, torch-bearer in the night, psychopomp, and mistress of magic. Anyone wanting to work with Hekate will gain from reading this book, whether they are new seekers on the path or witches of many moons. Teixeira offers forms of divination, spells, recipes and rituals blending historical research and her own experience as a high priestess, witch and herbalist dedicated to Hekate in her many guises.

Lucya Starza, author of Candle Magic, and Poppets and Magical Dolls

Pagan Portals

Temple of the Bones

Rituals to the Goddess Hekate

Jennifer Teixeira

MOON
BOOKS

Winchester, UK
Washington, USA

JOHN HUNT PUBLISHING

First published by Moon Books, 2021
Moon Books is an imprint of John Hunt Publishing Ltd., No. 3 East Street, Alresford
Hampshire SO24 9EE, UK
office@jhpbooks.net
www.johnhuntpublishing.com
www.moon-books.net

For distributor details and how to order please visit the 'Ordering' section on our website.

Text copyright: Jennifer Teixeira 2021

ISBN: 978 1 78904 282 5
978 1 78904 512 3 (ebook)
Library of Congress Control Number: 2020950305

A CIP catalogue record for this book is available from the British Library.

Design: Matthew Greenfield

UK: Printed and bound by CPI Group (UK) Ltd, Croydon, CR0 4YY
Printed in North America by CPI GPS partners

Contents

In Memory of Sunsmith

Introduction

There is no one definitive book that sets the guidelines for paganism and how you work magic or Honor the Goddess. The Temple of the Bones is a diverse group of Witches, who come together on the dark of the moon to work magic and honor the Mighty Queen Hekate from our heart and our bones. We are a ritual circle that includes people of all traditions and backgrounds, connected in sacred space through the worship of the Goddess. We understand, as Heraclitus said, that *there is nothing permanent except change.* The Goddess Hekate in her infinite power is a shapeshifter, keeper of mysteries, psychopomp to the dead and so much more. Not only do we seek out information that is available through books and the historic record, but also through personal work with the Goddess and daily practice. The writings in this book are Temple of the Bones Public rituals, my own personal workings, and other bits of things I have learned on my magical journey. It is my hope that they may help you on your own path to the Goddess.

This book was created in part for all of the members of the Temple and those interested in the temple, it is a historic record of ritual, how to create ritual for yourself through your own witchcraft practices. Maybe you have been curious but could never make it to the Temple. Perhaps you simply want this book to add to your collection of information on the practices of Dedicants to Hekate. Whatever your reason, here is a guide to these rituals.

Much of my experiences in Public Ritual are influenced by my High Priestess work with the Amazon Blood Mothers Coven, Starflower Coven, CAYA Coven, Grove of Hekate Full Moon Circle, Queen of Crossroads, Temple of the Bones, The Strophalos, Study with the Covenant of Hekate, and Familial Folk Magic. There have been bumps in the road, and I am grateful for this sacred space provided by the Goddess. I give my gratitude to The Titaness Hekate and all of my Teachers, Temples & Guides. Thanks go out to Rowan Rivers, my Temple Brother and fellow Dedicant of Hekate and to the Temple of the Bones we formed into being by acting on the words of the Goddess Hekate. From the Voice of Hekate and into your hands, here is the guidebook to rituals dedicated to the Mighty Queen and from The Temple of the Bones.

Thanks to all attendees of the Temple and to the Witches. Special Thanks to Rowan "Briar" Rivers for co-leading rituals alongside me every time, and to The Raven's Wing as our Hosts in Oakland and Portland, Robyn Scott Forbes for being a wise ally in ritual space, Akasha, Andrea, Barry, Grey, Mme. Bogart, Harold, Heather, Heaven, Iris, Irisanya, Jenny, Jon , Lisa, Manea, Nicki, Quetzal, Rha, Rune, Sharon, Sorita, Sunsmith, Yansumi, and all participants of The Temple of the Bones.

Foreword by Rowan "Briar" Rivers

Coming to the Crossroads

I certainly didn't plan to dedicate to Hekate. I don't think it really works that way with her. While I had been familiar with Hekate and had participated in circles dedicated to her, she had always hung out on the fringes of my awareness, present but out of focus. Until, suddenly, she was front and center.

I was going through a major change in my life. I'd just uprooted and moved from Los Angeles to the Bay Area, gotten married, found a new job that paid well, and started really investing in my magical training. Everything was going great. I found a magical shop less than a mile from my house and decided on a whim to drop by for a service to Hekate. I deeply enjoyed the ritual and was planning to attend again in the future, so you could imagine my surprise when I learned that the temple to Hekate was discontinuing their services and that I had attended the final one.

A new temple to Hekate would be taking their place, one of the store owners told me, and would I like to participate? I said yes, of course, and before I knew it, I was in charge of organizing and leading rituals that were open to the public. It was my first time in a leadership role within a magical community. To be honest, I didn't even know Hekate that well when I began, but within weeks I had gone from a sideline observer to a dedicated priestx. I wasn't sure I belonged in such a position, given the relative newness of my relationship with Hekate, but Hekate did not seem to share my doubts. It was not important that I hadn't chosen her - she had chosen me.

For two years I led these rituals, growing in my walk with the goddess from crossroad to crossroad. Eventually I left my job as a full-time theatre producer and went to work at the magic shop housing the rituals. I became a public representative of the triple-faced goddess and helped connect others to her awesome power every dark moon. I felt my witchcraft grow in profound, deep, and potent ways. I learned newer, more receptive ways of moving through the world that provided me with needed guidance, premonitions, and security. I began to own my power and claim my space in the world.

In her own amorphous way Hekate had gone from being on the periphery of my life to the center and circumference. As the months and years went on, I began to wonder whether or not my time being a public servant of Hekate was coming to a close. As I continued to develop my relationship with Hekate, I realized that the public rituals we were performing for her served the temple much more than they served me on a personal level. What was filling the cups of others was simultaneously draining mine. It was time once again for change.

This was really put to the test when, very suddenly, a devastating rip tore through our magical community, breaking friendships, splintering covens, and decimating careers. Seemingly overnight, massive amounts of toxic histories were exposed, battle lines were drawn, and sides were chosen. It was a time of great hurt for many people. For my part, I had almost no connection to any of the goings on, save that the person at the center of the scandal had been the very same person who encouraged me to start the new temple to Hekate. Ooh, that was messy for sure. Their fingerprints were all over our rituals: we sang their songs, used their invocations, followed their ritual format, and even deferred to them as the official "leader" - despite the fact that they were almost never in attendance and I did 90% of the work.

The allegations against this person were serious. Again, I found myself at the center of the crossroads. Do I take this opportunity to step back and focus on a more private relationship with Hekate, or do I move forward and offer my hurting community something newer and healthier for their spiritual paths? After discussing the matter with Bird, we decided that we would make a new temple, one that reflected the values and concerns of the people, and so Temple of the Bones was born.

At first, we were told that we could not do it. That we didn't have the right to make a new temple and that we could not honor the goddess in our own ways. This, of course, only cemented our resolve and added to our passion. It was a time of extreme liberation. How did we want to invoke the goddess? How did we want to divine in ritual to receive her guidance? What kinds of rituals would we do? Who would be allowed to lead? What format would we choose?

It took about a week of intense focus, discussion, and brainstorming but in the end, it came together with surprising clarity. Ultimately, we decided that we wanted to work with Hekate in many of her aspects and would choose a different aspect to invoke each month. We realized that we connected to her chthonic aspects strongly, and opted to abandon divination by tarot for divination by bones instead. It was important to allow our members to express their magical selves, and so whoever took the role of energetically cleansing the attendees could do so in whatever style they saw fit. We would encourage each attendee to connect with the dead by invoking their particular ancestors. We would allow anyone to take a ritual role who had participated three times, and we would widen our reach to include new people.

Out of the old guard who had been leading rituals to Hekate, only one person besides Bird and myself chose to stay. To say this was disheartening would be an understatement. But Bird and I had really put our hearts into this and we believed we were following the guidance of our goddess, and so we chose to move forward with faith in her and without fear.

Our first ritual was so widely attended we ran out of chairs. People loved the new format! They felt more connected to their ancestors. They quizzed us excitedly about the bones that they had drawn and began to study new forms of magic. It felt like we had really done something right. We had faced the crossroads and made a brave choice, and it had paid off. Not only were we providing the community with a much needed and deeply healing practice, we had also fashioned something meaningful that was personally fulfilling for us as well.

So, you see I never planned to work so closely with Hekate, to dedicate to her and build her a temple. That's just sort of the way it happened. Hekate has a way of catching you in moments of transition, of gently guiding you through signs and signals about which way to go. She is never pushy, never makes demands, she simply directs you with a passive, omniscient ambivalence and allows you to become more of who you are by choosing your own fate. By serving her I have served myself. And by letting her guide me at the crossroads I have carved my own path.

Here are some of the signs and symbols of Hekate that she may use to get your attention, direct your awareness, and lead you to greater heights of power and clarity.

Dogs: The animal the most closely associated with Hekate. With their strong senses of smell dogs may tune into things that are far off and out of our field of awareness. The barking of dogs announces the presence of Hekate and can indicate whether restless spirits are about.

Keys: As a goddess of liminal spaces, keys are very important to Hekate since they grant the ability to move from one place to another. Besides existing in the spaces between things (liminal spaces), Hekate is also a goddess of boundaries, and can force doors to lock and close if we are not ready to open them, or to keep danger out.

Crossroads: Both physical and metaphorical crossroads can be symbols of Hekate. She often appears to her followers when we are at a crossroads in life with insight to guide us on our journey. Offerings to her may be left at crossroads, and performing rituals to her in these spaces may add power to them.

Serpents: Constantly shedding their skin, snakes embody the process of death and rebirth sacred to Hekate. As a psychopomp who guides the souls of the dead to the Underworld and back, she is constantly treading the space between the living and the dead.

Shadow Work: Being confronted with an unpleasant aspect of yourself? That might be Hekate calling. Whether you're being forced to work on your fear, your prejudice, your insecurity, your temper, or self-medication, any time unseen aspects of yourself are brought forth to be reckoned with then Hekate is with you.

The Dead: As a chthonic deity, Hekate works closely with the dead. During the dark moon she is known to lead the souls of the restless dead up to the earth so that they may seek revenge or whatever they need for their souls to find peace.

Poison: As a mistress of poisons, Hekate guides us on how what may appear baneful can also be healing, and how what seems innocent can secretly be poison. She embraces the subtle arts, and may call on us to use cunning tactics and esoteric knowledge to achieve our means.

The Dark Moon: This is the time of month when feasts are traditionally set out for Hekate and the restless dead in an event called *Deipnon*. Usually consisting of three parts, the Deipnon involves setting a meal out for Hekate and her undead hosts, atoning for egregious behaviour/cleansing the self, and also cleansing the home.

Torches: Hekate is famously known for helping to guide the way, illuminating things hidden and revealing unseen paths. She can offer light in the darkness, and with her three faces turned to each direction there is nothing she cannot see. Turning to her for guidance can reveal essential information and emotional security as we walk our individual paths.

Garden of Souls

In my early experience as a solitary practitioner, I discovered her energy, at the time she was nameless, coming in different forms, pulling me out of the darkness that I swam in. I would offer her ecstatic dances, speak to her and allow her to pull me through the emptiness of time. In the years that followed she told me her name and once again another world opened up, where I would connect with others who have been chosen by the Titaness Hekate. Once I had learned the ways of Public Priestesshood, I was initiated by the light of Her Torches. Learning the Mystery and acknowledging the shared experience of all life. Temple of the Bones is you; you are connected to the Earth through your body, your bones like the stones, connected to your ancestors, your flesh the soil, blood and lymph are the rivers flowing, your passion and desire are the fires that light your path, the air you breathe and the words you speak are the essence of connection.

Hekate is often called a "Dark Goddess" as she walks through the shadows allowing for illumination by her torchlight. Hekate is the light emerging from the darkness, her light is there, guiding, opening doors and revealing the path ahead. Her transformative power is within the void, absorbing, just as the dark of the moon allows for release, her door is open, and lessons from the dark are her realm. It is time to allow her to guide you through your own transformation.

Hekate is the midwife of life, death, and rebirth. She is with us at all of these moments, offering her lessons, her blessings and her protection. There are many things we take on in this life, we consume, we create and destroy, and she helps guide us through the process. In the transition of bringing this Temple to being, we dealt with the pain of loss, and the beauty of rebirth. The death and decay only helps us to flourish, as the bones of our ancestors nourish the roots we tend to. Our energy and workings guided by Hekate allow for this transformation. The fruits of your labor and medicine can grow within the soil, the power they have can be used to nourish the body and soul.

In the dark we sleep as the moon is over us with her mysterious light. Our intuition and more primal instincts are at the surface, waiting to be harnessed. She is the balance of light and dark throughout the moon cycle. In ancient texts, Hekate is seen as the Maiden, with the wisdom of being fresh from the Underworld. She is Triplicate and a Goddess of the doorway to the Chthonic Realm.

Epithets of Hekate

Each month we focus on working with Hekate in one of her specific facets using one of her Epithets. We do this to add power to each working by choosing what we are focusing on. Having a specific goal in mind allows us to have better chances of success. Hekate is often seen as triplicate, and she walks with you at the crossroads, however, you cannot sit at the crossroads forever, you must choose which path you will walk on. Here is a list of a few Epithets to the Goddess and their meanings.

Phosphoros - Light bearer
Anassa Enodia - Queen of the Dead
Kthonia - Of the Underworld
Tridotis - Of the 3 ways
Soteira - Savior
Brimo - The Angry One
Trimorphos - 3 formed
Astrodia - Of the stars
Apotropaia - She that protects
Trioditis - Of the crossroads
Klêidouchos - who holds the keys
Propolos - she who serves
Krokopeplos - Of the Saffron Cloak
Einodia - Of the Path

Our rituals revolve around a large central working which shifts from month to month. From Dark Moon to Dark Moon we have been gathering petitions from the public altar room at The Raven's Wing Magical Company in Oakland, California. This is a prayer service the Temple of the Bones does for the Community, to help guide answers to all and offer protection and healing.

To begin the ritual, the heart beat drum takes us outside, We process outside with our Statue of Hekate to burn petitions to release them to the Goddess. Burning is done in the community cauldron with drums, rattle, and/or low humming and chants outside on the front stoop. Upon reentering, all are cleansed with cleansing herbs and given a tea light candle to use later in ritual for the ancestor invocation.

Casting the Circle in
The Temple of the Bones

This Portion of Ritual is done in many different ways, though we cast the Circle to protect attendees and remind us that we are now stepping into ritual space, this can be done how you choose. Hekate is a protectress and destroyer, she will offer safety just as strongly as she can direct daemonic forces to attack those who seek to harm her children. I will list a few ways that the circle is cast here.

Passing the Skull: In our circle we have a human skull replica we cover with a veil and pass around the circle for each attendee to hold and look into its "eyes" as a reminder that life is uncertain, that we will soon be as our beloved dead. "*We are all connected, We will all one day meet death*" Each person looks into the skull as it is passed around the circle. "*Death is inevitable, change is inevitable, Our planet is a Temple of Bones, in this place we experience the vision of the World. As holders of the Key we unlock the doorway to our path on the crossroads in times of chaos. As Torchbearers, It is up to us to carry on the fires from the Embers of destruction to light the Path and see the way. Like the Snake, we shed our skin and become new again.*"

The Garlic: The lead witch in charge of this activity should have more heads of garlic ready if needed. Cast a circle around the workspace using the head of garlic. Each person can take a clove of garlic off the head and hold on to it to give as an offering to Hekate later after she is invoked into the space. Move deosil, in a clockwise motion, saying, "*We are protected, within this circle*"

By Blade: One Witch leads the circle cast by blade, Typically in a clockwise fashion to create a container of energy and a circle of trust.

Elements of Hekate

This is used to Invoke the Elements and/or to prepare a cauldron for Divination (Scrying) or Creating Herbal Oils/Waters: Use common sense when working with herbal oils: Do not ingest, Do not use on animals or small children, and absolutely do not put in any orifice that may be sensitive to this kind of thing.

By the power of 3 X 3

You will need:

Base oil (Almond oil): Almond is a tree native to the Mediterranean and is sacred to Hekate.

Mugwort: *Artemisia Vulgaris* (Incense, Herb and Essential Oil) Cleansing and Used for prophecy. Dream enhancement and astral travel.

Wormwood: *Artemisia Absinthium* (Herb and Essential Oil) Used to protect one's space and self. It is used to reverse curses and send them back from where they came.

Peppermint: *Mentha Piperita* (Herb) Used to drive away negative entities and provide protection and clearing.

Rue: *Ruta Graveolens* (Herb) Protection from the "evil eye" or jealous thoughts and actions of others that may affect your advancement.

Dandelion: *Taraxacum Officinale* (Herb) Connects to Hekate's chthonic aspects. Aids in communication from the dead. Ancestral connection.

Cypress: *Cupressus sempervirens* (Essential Oil) The tree is evergreen, lives long and has a connection to the beloved dead. This plant is comforting when there is loss of a loved one, and can aid in communication with the divine.

Vetiver: *Vetiveria zizanioides* (Essential Oil) Helps to overcome poverty, Helps to process grief and promotes restful sleep.

Vetiver is grounding, calming and can repel thieves.

Lemon Verbena: *Aloysia Citrodora* (Herb) Breaks Bad habits and removes Malevolent Spells.

Using the herbs mentioned, combine into your cauldron or other suitable receptacle. You will let them steep from dark moon to dark moon undisturbed and never exposed to light. Use this oil during dark moons as a multipurpose ritual oil dedicated to the Service of Goddess Hekate.

By Heaven, Earth and Sea ~ I call to her powers of Heaven and of Air, of the sacred incantation and communication between the void ~ By smoke and fire I fumigate my cauldron, and bless it by the light of Hekate ~ (Use Mugwort Fumigation to Bless the Cauldron with the energy of Air) *I call to her powers of Earth and Herbs ~ That her wisdom be bestowed on these workings, granting wealth and healing ~ With these herbs I add to my cauldron, and bless it by the light of Hekate ~* (add the herbs to Inspire the energy of Earth) *I call to her powers of Sea and Divination ~ of the visions that come, for prophecy of the future, I call on my powers of intuition and knowing ~ With this water (or oil) I add to my cauldron, and bless it by the light of Hekate ~* (add your Almond Oil to make the Temple of the Bones oil or water for scrying and to call on the energy of water)

Ancestors of Blood and Affinity

Have you ever felt like you are not alone? That there is someone, or something in the room with you when you feel there should be no one? This can sometimes bring on a feeling of fear, or comfort, depending on what or who it is. When we speak of the energy of ancestors and ghosts, we come to understand that the presence of ghosts can be caused by various events. Typically, we see violent death and/or mistreatment as one of the main reasons for a haunting. There are beings that are restless and they attach themselves to persons or places. There is so much suffering in the world, having competency in the realm of ghosts can benefit yourself as well as to help heal the world around you. Ancestors can be ghosts, but not all ancestors are ghosts. Ghosts may want something from you that you are not willing to give, often it is your beautiful body, for they no longer have theirs. In these cases, we have the restless spirit that needs to be handled swiftly even in the face of terror. She is the Guide to lost souls, spirits and the restless dead, sometimes revealed in dreams and visions. They come to you with their stories. The feelings I get from these souls are intense and their narratives are vivid. In one instance I was visited by a woman who wanted my body, she wanted to tell me her experience. In this moment she had taken me back to where she was beaten, assaulted and killed. She wanted to take over my body. When I asked her where her body was, she told me it was eaten by dogs. I was paralysed and I felt hands holding me down, unable to scream or move, I could only speak to this spirit with my mind. This spirit never told me her name, and I was firm in my boundaries that she could not have my body. I reminded her that she did not deserve this and needed to move on now or else be in the eternal loop of restlessness and unease. Later on, I felt called to look up the story of the Biblical Jezebel, and her story felt eerily similar to that of the visitor in my sleep. Whether or not it was Jezebel, the story is not isolated to one culture or place. As Hekate is a guide, I ask her for help in the ease of these deaths and cruelty that seem to visit this earthly realm so often. I ask for protection and peace in my workings with these energies and the blessings to have the strength to help when I can. How do we all relate to our "Blood"? The ancestral and physical blood we spill in this earthly realm? Hekate reminds us that we all come from the deep cave of the womb. We emerge screaming and bloody into a world that is full of a variety of challenges. We have the tools we need to be successful on whatever path in the crossroads we decide to walk on.

Activities involving ghosts can include house cleansing and blessings, seances, soul retrieval, rituals of transformation, memorials, Deipnon and so on. The most common request I see is for the cleansing of homes. Often there is uncertainty about the tenants who have lived in a place before you. Sometimes it is of places that are thought to be haunted by several ghosts all at once. Also, there is the alternative that you have come into contact with a guardian of a certain place and your behaviour or activities do not fall in line with their expectations. If it is the former, you can cleanse your home and celebrate Deipnon, and that will most likely help, if it is the latter, then you may have a case of a guardian and you will need to look into what you are doing that is upsetting the guardian. Sometimes cleaning the house is all you need; other times the guardian may be offended by words you say in its presence. Is there a person who is living or working in the same space that has toxic behaviour? Think of why a guardian will be called into a place. It is usually because of some trauma that was felt in the area by sentient beings of this Earth. Guardians can be sensitive to screaming, destruction, foul language, violence and anything that you may call protection for. They are as different as people, and usually they make themselves known. For example, In a shop I worked at, an employee was lighting candles and honoring victims of homicide due to transphobia and bigotry in a group ritual. This person also slandered the girlfriend of a fellow employee who happened to be transgendered, and telling her employee that transgender women were all kinds of horrible things and she was clearly jealous of her. Soon the energy in the store had shifted, there was angry energy, items literally flew off the shelves when there was no reason for them too. Shelves fell off the walls that had been there for years with no issues. Accidents seemed to happen a little more frequently. Not long after, the woman who had been a hypocrite to the spirits was released from employment and asked to never return to the shop again. After this person and their indiscretion had been removed, things went back to normal.

Guides are psychic aides and/or teachers, who watch over and protect. They may have been with you from childhood, or they may be someone you picked up from another person or place. Typically, they choose who they help and come in contact with. Guides will help you choose the right components to create herbal remedies, help match you with the right Goddess and even help you get to know people who can further your goals in this life. Some of the ways people will contact their guides is through the use of tarot, pendulums or other tools of divination. Your guides will inspire action in your life, whisper in your ear and tell you when a situation is dangerous or when you are on the right track. This is similar to how you may connect with a benevolent ancestor. This could also be through guided meditation, dreams and different types of divination. Your guides can sometimes be subtle, or sometimes feel as though they have hit you with a hammer. You will know them by the lessons that they teach you. Did you hear them tell you to not do something and you didn't listen? Did they tell you to move forward but you stood still in fear, missing an important opportunity? You learn to listen to this as time goes on and you learn to let your guide do the work within you to move you forward. Understand, as well, that as time goes on, you build psychic muscle with daily practice, meditation and your work with self. This is why daily practice is important, you cannot lift 100 pounds overnight, but with everyday training, you will hit your mark with patience and dedication. Daily practice is so important to building magical muscle, and it can help you determine if you have a true ally in your guide or if it is a trickster energy.

Ancestor reverence is a key point in Temple of the Bones. Who are these ghosts that we feed on Deipnon? They are not deities; they travel through layers of existence led by the Mighty Hekate. They visit us in the physical world. As transient as they seem, oftentimes, it is the space we are in, a tragic event that keeps them held in an area, or a feeling so strong that it holds space. In our work with Hekate we encourage the release of this accumulated energy that has been stagnant and festering. Following this ancient Goddess into the dark, we ask for benevolence and release of our own pain and suffering. We wish for all souls to receive the peace they need by the light of Hekate's' Torches.

When we call in Ancestors, we ask each attendee to light a candle at the Altar of Hekate, and say out loud the name of one beloved ancestor. The first person to lead this portion brings the memory of one esteemed ancestor to the altar, a person who has recently passed, a well-loved teacher, or someone well known in the community for their life's work. Often it is an ancestor of affinity, one that we relate to, but is not necessarily of close blood relation. It can be any of these, all of these, or none of these, it is up to the witch in charge of this portion and is brought to the attention of the witches they will circle with for approval. After the esteemed ancestor of the community is honored, each attendee brings their tealight candle to the altar, and they say the name of their own beloved ancestor and a few words about them out loud or in silence as they light the candle.

All ancestors are welcomed by a *"Hail and Welcome"* when they enter the circle.

Calling the Goddess

In the Temple of the Bones we typically did not have things written down to recite from. You are expected to go on the month-long journey to find Hekate and speak of her in the circle, educating and perhaps reminding those in ritual with you who Hekate is and how she wishes to be honored. That being said there are invocations of Hekate that are written out, but if you plan to hold a ritual to The Mighty Queen, you will absolutely need to be kept up to date on her energy. Speaking your heart through your voice, either by chant or enunciated and loud enough for all to hear, is a good skill to have in ritual space. In this book, there are some sample ritual outlines and formats that have more details on these sample invocations, some are unique to the temple and some are from historic accounts.

If you are given the honor of calling in Hekate for ritual, I would suggest familiarizing yourself with her stories and energy. You can be a bard, reciting the stories of Hekate and her Magic, You can look into her specific Epithet, and go into more detail about what it means and how it is focused. You can recite an invocation taken from history, or come up with your own. When you are done you greet her with a *"Hail and Welcome!"* Keep in mind that if you call her in, you will be expected to give her a *"Hail and Farewell"* at the end of ritual as well.

After Hekate is called into the circle, she is given offerings from the attendees and witches of the circle. In an historical context, Hekate enjoyed offerings of garlic, wine, honey, red mullet, and round honey cakes. In the Temple of the Bones when calling in the Titaness Hekate, we offer her what is available locally, things like wine, cheese, almonds, olive oil, garlic, eggs, honey, bread and just about anything we will be enjoying during cakes and ale. Sometimes attendees will bring her gifts for the altar, and they will remain in the altar box for rituals or a Ritual

Witch will leave the item in the Labyrinth or Crossroad for Hekate when the ritual is done, or as Hekate requests.

The Ritual Working

Ritual is an activity that was given to us by the cycles of the universe. The Earth travels around the sun giving us the gifts of our Sabbats and Seasons. The Moon travels around the Earth Giving us our Moon Cycle. These have been with us from the beginning and are the same solar bodies that the ancients gazed upon in wonder for thousands of years, acting out rituals for the releasing and receiving of the benefits of the Universe.

Urban witches learn the lessons early in a life of solitude. There is a skill in creating safe space for mental relaxation on busy streets and packed hallways. There is also a skill in being present and being fully aware of your surroundings, as it is paramount to safety in a fast-moving world. How to be in a meditative calm state, but also be aware of the people and places around you is a valuable skill in keeping yourself safe and sane.

Intention is a powerful tool in creating rituals that work, but intention is not everything. If you are calling on Hekate you want to have a clear focus on what her energy is and what she will want to help you with. The same goes for what the herbs and plants are used for magically, and how May Apple *Podophyllum peltatum* is not always the best substitute for True Mandrake *Mandragora Officinarum*.

Intention is an important tool, as it gives us the vision of what we want and allows us to focus on acquiring that result. Utilizing the proper elements and energies are important to creating successful workings. Intention is important as a guideline with how you put together spells and create ceremonies. It is oftentimes the focus of the magic; you want a particular result. It is your vision for the spell that you desire. Again, I mention **Focus as Intention and Vision.** You follow this path and your ceremony or spell has ingredients and actions that inspire results. Having the clarity of what you want and how to get it are essential to success in life and magic. This is how the two; success in life and magic can help guide you. **Focus.**

Alchemy is defined typically as the process of turning lead into gold, but has anyone ever literally done it like that? How do you create the magic of transformation? How do you bring something that has been unsuccessful to something that is labeled as success? You need to look at the elements that are not allowing for success and remove them, then you will gain more insight on **what is the success** of the spell. How does it inspire your action? What elements are you incorporating into your workings? Your witchcraft is a **Practice**, you are constantly trying to improve your work, but in order to do that, you need to **do the work.** Ask yourself: Once Hekate is with you in the circle how do you wish to honor her? What is it you need her help with? Is the Goddess Hekate and Her Epithet in alignment with your goal and purpose of the ritual?

The Bone Oracles

Practice for Divination

In the Temple of the Bones Ritual Circle to Hekate we have our set of Divinatory "Bones". These are blessed and borrowed from Temple Witch Briar for the purpose of this public circle. At the end of each ritual, attendees are guided to pull a bone from the cauldron and to see what their message is. This simple activity is intended to access awareness of such an object, to trigger the mind that, already in a state of connection, would bring out messages that could further bless that individual's path. Psychic awareness is not easy to access for everyone, but within ritual, we look for the signs that the Goddess Hekate has signs or messages that allow us to access images that may help us on the path.

Once you have fully connected to your own psychic awareness you may no longer need the triggers to your powers of divination, you still may like them and enjoy the use of such, but it is the power of your mind that can translate the messages from the future. Meditation and relaxation can allow for an open mind, one that is protected and aware. This Bone divination Guide was written for the Temple of the Bones by Rowan Rivers.

Bone Divination Guide : Temple of the Bones

Bone reading is an ancient form of divination practiced by dozens of cultures from all over the world. While styles and methods can differ greatly, most contemporary bone readers use a set of tools including bones, shells, herbs, crystals, and other natural curios. Bone reading is ancestral. Our ancestor's DNA survives within us, and the animals, plants, and rocks of this earth all stretch far back into time to connect us to the source of all life. In this sense, all life is one family. This is a brief guide and introduction into the symbolism of certain bones. Use it to contemplate the messages, questions, and warnings that certain pieces may have for you. Many of these items were found and many donated by witches of the Temple with the original set coming from Rowan Rivers personal collection. This is a guide to what the pieces in our temple mean, each piece has a story, where it was found, and under what circumstances all determine its meaning. Think of this when creating your own bone set.

Fossilized Shell: The importance of maintaining traditions, honoring our roots, and guarding the home against outsiders. Protect your precious inheritance by respecting your heritage.

Raccoon Baculum: The need to connect with others, be seen, and have meaningful relationships. Sacred sex. Beware mansplaining or taking up too much space.

Fulgurite: Sudden bursts of inspiration, intense processing. Handle high energy with care, allow yourself to be transformed, and be sure that inspiration does not leave as quickly as it came.

Alligator Claw: Hold onto that which is truly needed, let go of that which serves ego but neglects spirit. Your ancestors are trying to get your attention.

Sunstone: Your inner nature must shine forth. Embrace your passions, explore your talents, and let go of artificial identities. You must lead by example now.

Ebony Shard: Deep shadow work. The healing of ancestral trauma is of great importance. Strength under pressure.

Nutmeg: Sweetness and enjoyment of life are necessary! Enjoy the good, but remember that too much sweetness can spoil the stomach. Neither deprive nor over-indulge.

Petrified Wood: Focusing on alignment is of great importance right now, physically, spiritually, internally and externally. Return to nature to remain centered, rooted, and strong.

Coyote Claw: Use every ounce of cunning and strategy that you have in order to achieve your goals. Be prepared for every possible outcome and you will not be caught off-guard.

Abalone Shell: Now is the time to foster your spiritual gifts. Explore your talents. You have the right container in which to foster them, make use of it.

Ball of Lead: Roll with the punches while remaining grounded. You may be hung up on something. Be adaptable while finding what sustains you. Let go of heavy emotional baggage.

Lodestone: Be very conscious of what you are attracting into your life right now. Luck is following your suggestions, whether conscious or unconscious, good or bad.

Sunflower Seed: Become a source of light in the world and evil will not be able to plague you.

Hematite: Remain balanced and grounded, detox and honor your body. Deal with stress in healthy ways.

Snake jaw: Remain guarded but non-aggressive. Defend yourself when called for but do not abuse your power. Send silent signals to let others know if they are crossing lines.

Pyrite: Focus on material prosperity right now! Money is important- make the most of it.

Tourmaline: Guard, protect, and defend yourself at all costs. Negative energies must be averted. Your home should be fortified, and make sure you are getting enough nutrition.

Red Jasper: Pay attention to your physical and emotional health. Reduce emotional stress to bolster your constitution.

Coyote Tooth: Cleverness and attention are your friends right now. Beware wordplay and mind the details. You need not disclose everything if it makes you vulnerable, but stay honest.

Black Rock: Stay grateful for the ordinary things in life. Appreciate the little things and your wealth and happiness will grow.

Buckeye: You are lucky! Don't take gratuitous risks, but go for good chances. The odds are on your side.

Broken Larimar: Emotional healing is the focus. Let go of past pain and flow into a healthier future. Keep a cool head and your struggles will wash away like the river.

Rattlesnake Rattler: Let others know if they are treading on you. Radical self-defense.

Fossilized Stingray Barb: Over defensiveness triggered by past circumstances. Examine your triggers and seek healing spaces.

Cubeb Berry: Celebrate your creative, sexual, ecstatic nature! Participate in joy, even if it is for a moment.

Balm of Gilead Bud: Seek out reconciliation where you have unresolved conflict. This will heal you.

Red Tiger Eye Cube: If you remain poised and powerful nothing can overcome you.

Moonstone: Flow with the rhythms in your life right now, looking to nature for guidance. Honor the wisdom of respected women in your life. Listen to your dreams. Heal by letting go.

Black Cobra Pellet: Dispose of teachings and practices which are no longer of use to you.

Cat's Eye Shell: Spirit is speaking to you! Look for signs and patterns all around you.

Blue Kyanite: Messages are trying to come through from someone far away. Empathy, curiosity, and art will guide you towards your destiny.

Snake Vertebrae: Remain flexible on details, but do not compromise on your direction.

Fluorite Octahedron: There are many sides to an issue. Quiet your mind, focus, and you will be able to see both the forest and the trees.

Cat Ankle Bone: Achieve your potential by staying mobile! Envision the heights of your success, then apply your skill and will in order to achieve them.

Snake Rib: Things may seem too large to handle, but if you do your best to make space for them you will be able to process much more than you believe.

Snowflake Obsidian: There is light in the dark. Protect yourself but refrain from warfare. Your ability to self-heal and reject negativity will confound your enemies and inspire your friends.

Sodalite: Remain open to higher perspectives by applying yourself to learning. Additional insight may benefit you greatly now. Don't be afraid to teach those who come to you to learn.

Iron Nail: Apply focus and will to obtain your goals. Do not bend to others, remain strong in your resolution. You are holding together more than you know. Ancestral gifts.

Bone Mala Bead: Pray to and work with your ancestors right now to clear the path and achieve your best possible outcome. Daily work with your spirits is encouraged.

Key: Now is the time to explore the unexplored. Awaken your potential, discover new possibilities, and reject limitations. You can overcome your obstacles.

Broken Black Glass: Be on guard. Someone does not have your best interests at heart, but they cannot hurt you in serious or lasting ways.

Eel River Glass: Let the world soften and reshape you. Places of resistance within you are being fashioned into places of gentility, beauty, and clarity. Rediscover something you'd written off.

Arm with Torch: (from a broken statue of Nike) You must lead by example because others are looking to you for guidance.

Great personal strength will be called for. Endurance and integrity are your winning graces.

Bat Nut: Do not be afraid of your strangeness. Your unique qualities offer you power and protection. Evil forces will not avail you.

Lost Quartz Point: Reunification. Not all that is absent is lost. A journey is about to be completed.

Healed Bone: Recovering from trauma is a process, but at the end of your recovery you will become stronger in the places that have been broken. Do not despair.

Shark Tooth: Go to the beach and give your troubles to the ocean. While you must keep moving you must also find rest. Do not move backwards!

Snail Shell: Look in simple places for evidence of the goddess. Cosmic mysteries lie very close to home at this time. Make sure your spiritual structures and your day to day life support each other.

Coyote Vertebrae: Look out! Trickster energy is about! For answers you must look within. Stay flexible in your understanding. Illusions and riddles surround you.

White Stone: Prioritize a daily spiritual practice at this time. Consistency, dependability, and stability are important spiritual qualities to focus on. Let your devotion be simple and persistent.

Lost Button (Found Button): Hidden treasures are waiting for you. Engage your sense of discovery.

Offerings

Jason was told by Medea to propitiate Hekate *"pouring from a goblet of hive soaked labour of bees."* Honey was known as a "Sober Offering" as round honey cakes, drinks, and more. Hekate has guided Persephone from the depths of Hades, and brought her back to be with her mother, and in turn Spring comes to the cold and dark earth. The connection between mother and daughter is Hekate. The first flowers of spring bring sustenance back to the Earth and reflect the emotion of Demeter on her daughters return.

Honey has been used as an offering to deities across the globe, when we think of how much work it can take to create a teaspoon of honey. (It takes 12 worker bees a lifetime to make a teaspoon of honey!) You can see what dedication, time and focus the teaspoon of honey can represent. It is a powerful ingredient in any work involving attraction, chthonic aspects, career, and healing. It is the nectar of a million flowers that can be present in that little teaspoon.

- **How does it work to Attract?** Honey is sweet and sticky, it flows slowly, but it grabs onto what it touches. It can make a mess if not handled properly.
- **How is it chthonic in nature?** In the wild, bees often create their hives in caves or hidden and dark places. This makes it a good offering to Hekate who is seen as a Goddess that can travel between the worlds. If you see "wild foraged honey" it is especially good to get as an offering to her.
- **How does it Create meaningful work?** The worker bees, guided by the queen are a powerful representation of female empowerment. The queen bee is fertile and in charge. The worker bees are all female and they are the

protectors and nurturers of the hive, they are guided by the queen.

- **How does it help in healing?** Honey is used to help with sore throats, coughs, and in topical applications to prevent infection. An elixir made with honey can be used internally to ward off colds, help prevent allergies, warm the body and can give you energy.

Hekate's Herbal Honey

1 teaspoon cinnamon powder
1 tablespoon fresh peeled and grated ginger
A pinch of saffron
4 ounces raw honey (preferably Wild Foraged or Tomb Honey)
4 ounces brandy (optional)

Make some for Hekate and some for yourself, as it is always nice to share and will better connect you to her. Allow the mixture to blend for a full moon's cycle before enjoying. Add a spoonful to hot water or tea to help soothe a sore throat or provide enjoyment.

Add all the food ingredients together and mix till combined. Give the offering to Hekate, and ask for her help on your path, may the rewards be sweet!

The Earth began to bellow, trees to dance
And howling dogs in glimmering light advance
Ere Hekate came. The Aeneid, book VL. Virgil.

Cakes and Ale

Hekate's Honey Cake

1 cup honey
½ cup sliced almonds

¼ cup poppy seed
2 cups all-purpose flour
½ teaspoon baking soda
½ teaspoon salt
½ teaspoon cardamom powder
¼ cup butter
4 duck eggs (or 4 chicken eggs if duck is not available)
¼ cup plain yogurt

Grease a 9-inch springform pan while the oven preheats at 325 degrees. Sprinkle half of the almonds onto the bottom of the pan. In one bowl mix the dry ingredients, in another bowl, mix the eggs, butter, and honey. Add the dry ingredients to the wet, mix, then add the yogurt. Pour into the prepared 9-inch springform pan, cook at 325 for approx. 50-60 minutes.

Kykeon

Kykeon is an ancient Greek beverage thought to be fermented and possibly psychotropic depending on what recipe was used, the main ingredient being Barley. A beverage related to the Eleusinian mysteries that is thought to have allowed for Divine Inebriation, a key to the doors of the otherworld and the mysteries of Eleusis. Archaeological evidence suggests this may have been a hallucinogenic substance with the addition of ergot infected grain. Perhaps it was simply a ritual beer, an alcoholic drink imbibed to break the required fasting before ceremonies. It is likely other herbs were used in the recipes, some possibilities include poppy, pennyroyal, henbane and thyme. These are some modern recipes used as ritual offerings and for cakes and ale.

Barley and Herb

1 cup pearled barley rinsed
Handful of fresh peppermint

2 quarts water
¼ cup honey

Combine water and barley into a pot to boil, once it is at a boil, reduce the heat, stir and simmer for approx. 30 minutes. After the barley is soft, turn off the heat and strain the barley from the water saving it for later use. Add the water to the mint and cover for five minutes. Strain the mint off, mix in the honey and enjoy. Barley water is a nutritious drink that is hydrating and enjoyable.

Kykeon ale

1 pound of pearled barley
1 gallon of water
2 ounces dried nettles
2 pounds of organic sugar
Ale yeast
Additional water to make 2 gallons.

Boil barley and water together till the barley is soft for approximately 30 minutes. Turn off the heat and add the nettles to the pot, covered for 10 minutes. Strain the liquid while hot enough to dissolve the sugar. Let it sit until a little warmer than room temperature. Add more water to make two gallons. Dissolve a ½ ounce of the yeast to a small amount of warm water, then add to the two gallons. Mix well. Then leave covered with a cheesecloth (tightly so no bugs can get in) for three days. It will be ready to drink then. You can substitute other herbs for the nettles or add lemon juice. Saffron, lemon balm, or rose might be a nice alternative, depending on what ritual you will be sharing this at. This one will get you intoxicated.

Caffè d'orzo

In a modern context it may be more practical to enjoy a roasted barley tea to break a fast or as a pre-ceremony drink. It is generally a lovely beverage if you enjoy the flavor of coffee. No caffeine, but the spices can warm you up in a cold world. This is an excellent fall and winter drink.

 2 Teaspoon roasted barley ground
 ¼ teaspoon nutmeg powder
 ¼ teaspoon cinnamon powder
 ¼ teaspoon cardamom powder
 1 teaspoon mushroom powder

Place everything except the mushroom powder in a french press, Pour over approximately eight ounces of hot water and let steep for 10 minutes. Gently compress the barley and spices and pour into a cup, add the mushroom powder and milk and honey to taste. The mushroom powder will settle to the bottom, but you will want to drink the powder for the added benefits. I made this for a friend and she affectionately called it "Hekate's Pumpkin Spice" To which I was not amused.

 O Lord Helios and Sacred Fire
 The spear of Hekate of the Crossroads
 Which she bears as she travels Olympus
 And dwells in the triple ways of the holy land
 She who is crowned with oak-leaves
 And the coils of wild serpents.
 The Root Cutters, Sophocles

Spells and Witchcraft

Every day spellwork is essential to building magical muscle and feeling confident in public ritual. This starts with a daily practice, meditation, sauntering in nature, writing in your Grimoire, or praying at the altar of Hekate to start and/or end the day. This is simple, take an hour of your day to do one or more of these things. You can be creative, many witches like to write out a daily prayer that they use to remind themselves of the power they hold within themselves, and it is a good way to have a consistent practice even when you are not feeling the free flow prayer coming to your lips. The Great Goddess Hekate is a Goddess of Witchcraft, and the practice of it will connect you to Her.

Some Examples of a daily practice:

#1

Movement: Reach to the sky

Prayer: *My mind is free and open*

Movement: Bring hands down to head slowly

Prayer: *A singing well*

Movement: Hands to heart

Prayer: *My heart is calm and respectful, A kettle drum*

Movement: Arms out

Prayer: *My arms are an illusion*

Movement: Float arms down

Prayer: *Darkness before the dawn*

Movement: Hands to belly

Prayer: *My belly is soft and rounded, a simmering cauldron*

Movement: Hands to hips, begin to sway or shimmy hips

Prayer: *My hips are warm and expressive, a flickering candle*

Movement: Hands down reaching toward the ground but you stand tall

Prayer: *My legs are strong and balanced, pillars of the Earth*

#2

Light candle and say:
Life is a gift that I have been given,
I manifest Joy and understanding in those around me,
I arise to heal and protect my loved ones,
For I am a healer of all wounds

#3

At Your Altar to Hekate say:
I live in my truth and speak with love,
I am a child of Hekate,
When I hear her wisdom, I listen.
When I seek her truth, I learn.
My gratitude is unending.
I have so much to be grateful for.

Even if you are planning on free flow prayer It is important to write down or have a print out of your daily practice, so even on days when you feel less than inspired, you can commit to something you wish to be blessed with each day. The best practice is one you have custom made for your life and your goals. On another note, if you focus on one thing, this is more likely to happen. You are praying for this every day.

Deipnon

The Deipnon, the supper to honor and appease the restless dead and cleanse the household, is traditionally done at the new moon once a month. This is the time when Hekate leads the spirits of the unavenged up from the underworld. Purification of the home is has done during this time and as it is the new moon, it is a good time to release and honor the experience of the past. In our workings, in our modern temples dedicated to Hekate, we offer food to the restless dead and open up the doorway to honoring them through sharing their legacy. We see injustice every day and we tend to desensitise ourselves to the cruelty; we become apathetic and hard. Gathering together in community, we share our energy, share our food together and get to know each other. Through Hekate we look to those who have been taken too early, and look to their work to see what must be done to appease their spirit. Offerings of eggs, herbal honey and other sacred foods that may be related to the restless dead are left at the crossroads.

To celebrate Deipnon, first cleanse your altar space and fumigate the area with herbs. Typically, this would be incense prepared specifically with this working in mind. Mugwort bundles are a good herb to use for this as well. Mugwort is used for consecration and opening the mind for divination. A little bundle of fresh mugwort dipped in water and sprinkled around the room is also appropriate for cleansing if smoke is not an option. Cast your circle with the herbal smoke or water. This will allow for focus and protection during this Deipnon.

Gather the names of those who died in your area that have been killed unjustly. Make an ancestor altar dedicated to them. Place pictures and/or their names on your altar. In our own Temple we have found that there have been many people in our community that have been killed for being different reasons or are targeted due to bigotry. These souls often remind us of ourselves, as we have found in our workings with the public, those who are called to Hekate are on the edges of society, they are often feral and wild. Inside of us exists a tender-hearted side and yet there is no taming of us. Call to these souls, say their names out loud and honor their life and experience. Demand justice for them, describe any details you can about them and hail them, welcome them.

Call to Hekate Anassa Eneroi, Queen of the Dead. Give her praise and honor her. Bring offerings to her at this time. Light her a candle and sit in silence with her for the lives lost. Say their names again, this time bid them a Hail and Farewell, may this journey be better than the last.

Hail and Farewell to Hekate, may she live in our hearts and bless our path with her light. Open your circle, and once again cleanse the space.

After such a ritual, it is appropriate to make a donation to an animal shelter or offer help at a homeless shelter or some other space that helps those people who are unhoused, sick, or otherwise on the fringe.

Sometimes spirits or energy can come to you and they do not mean to help you achieve your highest good. They seek to siphon off your energy and can make you ill or lethargic. Again, this is sometimes from a person, a place or has followed you through your bloodline. This goes for curses, the evil eye and so on.

The evil eye is so simple, and can come from just about anywhere at any time in your life. You are likely to have given the evil eye to someone else unknowingly, it comes from inner turmoil of the self and the feeling of lack that most of us have when we see someone who has what we want. The better you are at controlling your own evil eye the better you will be at controlling other eyes on you. Again, this is all in practice, you will get better if you keep on trying. It is a bit of resistance that can keep us moving forward, failure can seek to stop us in our tracks, but pushing forward can make the difference between getting what you want or standing still and being wounded from the hate in others. When you feel jealousy and anger rising in regard to another, sit with that feeling for a few moments. Allow yourself to feel it, and look at why you are feeling this way. What can you do to create a better life? Remember it is not obsessing over others, and what you perceive them to have. Release these feelings to Hekate and ask for her help in your own transformation, otherwise you just throw your energy into that other person, depleting your own power of transformation. An evil eye can fester into a curse, this is where you choose to place your energy into the destruction of another. It is significantly more powerful than the evil eye. Whether or not you believe in cursing, you will be handling an energy that is much more powerful than you, and allowing it into your space. Remember to Practice Safe Hex. That goes for love spells too.

It is important to find those people who encourage and inspire you. The muses in your life who will provide you feedback that is meant to serve you in achieving your highest good. Be aware that some people have both inspiration and will provide resistance. The resistance is a failure mentality within many of us, that we (or others who associate with us) are not as good or cannot do the work others are doing based on our situation, be it generational curses and/or social conditioning. If your value of self is weak, you may not be valuing those friends who choose to be in the circle with you. Sometimes we place our own inadequacy on others, if we truly valued our work, we would value that of our friends and community as well. People will often value a stranger's work more than that of an acquaintance or friend, and the saying "familiarity breeds contempt" is given life. Of course, there is also the other side of that coin, in which you place someone on a pedestal, and they fail to live up to the hype they or others have placed on themselves.

Here are some Moon workings you can do on your own to clear out negativity and strengthen your power.

Dark of the moon

During the dark of the moon, the void is open, absorbing and ready to consume what you give to it. This is a time that reminds us to look to our own void. What is the space that hides the vastness of your power? What lies deep within the Soul sleeping? Slumbering in its chrysalis? What is waiting for the ripening sun to burst through the amniotic fluid of emptiness? Think on what it is that you have kept from yourself, what powers have kept you from it and what it is you seek to one day harvest. The dark of the moon is a good time to commit to workings related to banishing, hexing, release, protection, underworld deities, Deipnon, mediumship and the dead. The Temple of the Bones public rituals are typically held in the dark of the moon, But Hekate can be worshiped anytime.

These are solitary rituals that can prepare you for working with the public.

Protect yourself

Tarot deck
Small tourmaline (or other protective stone)
Little bottle
Your choice of three protection herbs, Can be any combo of the following, or another herb you may have a connection to for protection that is not on this list~
Yarrow
Wormwood
Bay
Angelica root
Lemongrass
Isopropyl alcohol

Prepare your space by casting a circle. Pull out the Strength card from your tarot deck and place it at the head of your work area. Focusing on the energy of strength, interpret the Strength card by reading the tarot booklet and/or concentrating on the messages from the card. Ask the energy in the room what it is you should focus on for healing from fear in your life and pull out a random card from the tarot deck. Interpret the meaning of the card and place your bottle on top of the random card.

Begin to place your evil eyes, stones and then herbs all into the bottle focusing on what needs a little added protection (based on what the card revealed) in your life. Fill bottle ¼ with the alcohol then add water to fill to the top. Place this bottle on your altar to Hekate until the next dark moon. During this time, it is protecting the space around the altar, after the moon cycle you will use this as a hand wash for your workings and anything you do to help with your fears and move forward with courage.

Allow yourself to sit in a still and quiet place where you can feel the silence around you, sometimes this means finding the places between the noise to get a feeling of stillness. In a fire safe container (cauldron or metallic bowl) take a piece of charcoal and use the incense below as you think of the boundaries you have placed on yourself that are not serving and which ones you need to keep. Let go and release those that are deadweight on your flight into your future.

Dark of the moon incense

It is time to make room for the blessings to come. Scry into the smoke. Allow the smoke to float, and pay attention to the shapes of smoke, as messages will come to you.

Dark of the moon incense

Juniper berry, Styrax and Dragon's Blood Resin. (adding a few drops of blood to the incense can add a personal touch to the blend allowing for your DNA to be received into the offering.) This will be equal parts of each, but you can adjust as you like and with what you have.

Juniper berry, the look of this little fruit resembles the dark moon. It has a camphor like aroma and is a very clearing incense. It will break up hexes sent your way and protect you all the while. Crush up your Juniper berries in your mortar and pestle to release some of the aroma now. Take a good whiff! It is crisp, cutting and will bring out the essence of letting go of that which you do not need.

Liquidambar styraciflua/balsam or Styrax resin comes from The Styrax bush, often called benzoin, in this recipe you are using the liquid extract (though you could use the powder as a substitute) It has a sticky oozy consistency, and smells sweet. It is used to clear out evil energies, invite good luck and good allies. Styrax is a wonderful resin to offer to Hekate. It is mercurial in nature which will allow for ease in communication. Use it to invoke your power and walk with authority during this time.

Dragon's Blood Resin powder: Again, you can break out that mortar and pestle and release those big chunks of resin into a fine workable powder. Dragonsblood is a power enhancer, a fierce protector and Catalyst for the other resins in this blend.

Crush Juniper berries, add Styrax liquid resin, mix the Dragon's Blood Resin powder together and burn on charcoal in a heat safe dish during ritual.

Dark moon bath

You will need:

1 cup of black salt
Approx. 1 cup lemongrass herb
Powdered egg shell AKA Cascarilla (or a whole egg)
1 black candle

On the dark of the moon prepare a strong herbal tea of the lemongrass and be sure to save a teaspoon to make a herbal tea for yourself to drink after the bath. Strain the tea from the herb and begin to prepare your bath.

Start the water and place your black salt into the tub, add the lemongrass tea and as it begins to fill dip the cascarilla into the tub to get it wet and draw a pentacle on your belly. This will purify and protect by using the power of the pentacle and the cascarilla. Crumble the rest of the cascarilla into the bath water and light your candle. If using a whole egg, draw with the whole egg and leave in the tub unbroken, when done take the egg outside to a crossroad and break it there. You can look inside the egg for any signs or symbols that may further guide you in the results of your work.

Say a small prayer for yourself as you enter the bath, call on Hekate for protection. *"Hekate I ask of you, Transform any curses, evil and hatred that have been sent to me into energy I can use for my benefit, and anything that cannot be transformed be sent into the Earth to be recycled."*

Allow yourself to soak for at least 20 minutes. When you are done go and make your lemongrass tea to drink and think of what you can do to manifest what it is you need in your life now. (Let the candle burn all the way)

Cascarilla is traditionally used in folk magic to banish negative energies; it is powdered egg shell that has been formed into one solid piece and can also be used to write sigils on the body and concrete floors (like a chalk). The black salt can be the volcanic salt or any salt that is mixed with charcoal and sea salt. These are cleansing and purifying. Lemongrass is used to cut away evil, and it is something that you wash yourself in, but can also drink to help with better decision making on your part. This spell can also be used as a foot bath, if a full tub is not suited for your needs.

For protection

Use when dealing with difficult or stressful situations and to send back curses. Best used at the beginning of the dark or waning moon You will need:

A piece of Black Tourmaline
Rosemary, Clove and Lemon Verbena 1 teaspoon of each herb
1 cup of sea salt
A black candle
A bath tub or foot bath
Incense for protection made on the dark moon. (see Dark of the moon incense)

A muslin bag to place the herbs so not to get the tub dirty and not have to call a plumber. Or if using a foot basin, you can place the herbs in the water.

Censor and charcoal for incense.

Cleanse the tub before your work with the incense. And Recite the Following (or create your own):

I cast out negativity from my space,
I tell you now; Get Out of My Face!
Back to your master, whom you will fell,
And send your poisons back to hell.

(Note that this is a counter-attack protection spell, and is martial in nature. This is to send back a curse. If you wish to neutralize the curse, you can omit the above and create your own recitation for washing away attachments from others, ending with *"and it harm none"* Or use the preceding Dark moon bath)

Light your candle, begin to add the water, salt and herbs (in a muslin bag) to the bath, mixing them and reciting the above once again as you drag the tourmaline across your body from head to toe. Place the tourmaline in the bath.

As you lower yourself gently into the water, recite the incantations one more time. Bathe for at least 20 minutes, as you drain the water imagine the drain is taking away your stress and suffering as well. If you are using a movable basin, take it out of the home and release the water to just outside your home boundaries. Keep in mind that salt can kill plants when placed in the earth.

Dark moon amulet

You will need:

A skeleton key

red cording (thin like floss)
A black candle that will drip wax.

Cast a circle of protection around you and your space. Write this prayer down in your own writing and sign it at the end on a piece of paper small enough to wrap around the key:

I send back the curse; It is Broken!
My path is protected, the way will be open.
By the Power of Hekate's Key
You cannot beat me!

Light your candle. Say the prayer out loud as you wrap the neck of the key with the paper. Take the red cording and continue to chant it out as you drip wax on the paper. Begin to wrap the key in the red cord as you continue to drip wax on the cord. Wrap the key at least three times around (and preferably in multiples of three). Once you are finished, chant three more times and let the candle burn to completion. Place this key at or near your doorway for protection from those who seek to harm you and reverse curses sent your way.

The full moon

There is something about the watery orb of the night that is our moon. The Light of Hekate's Torches, like the full moon, unveils her secrets and shines light on your path. The intoxicating satellite fills our vision with its opalescence; it ignites the spark of night, exciting and opening us to the powers of manifestation. This inspiring torch in the frame of stars and darkness leads us to tunnels of energy that have been traveling in the otherworld of the void. We take sips of the elixir that is healing in nature and of the guidance that lets us voice our gratitude. In the acknowledgement of our source of pride and recognition, we utilize the reflection of this light to help shine on the path of manifestation.

Florida Water

In ritual we often used the Lanman/Murray Florida Water as an accelerant because of its availability and cost. Unfortunately, it is full of fragrances and colors. Here is a recipe that I have adapted from my good friend and fellow High Priestess, Quetzal. In order for this Agua de Florida to work for ritual, it needs to be high in alcohol.

You will need:

approx. 1 pint 80-100 % alcohol (Grain preferred)

Fill a jar with citrus peels, rose petals, mint, and cinnamon sticks. Cover with alcohol and bury it in the earth or place in a dark closet as close to the ground as possible for a full moon cycle. When you uproot it, strain the bulk matter out and decant the alcohol into an appropriate vessel. If you want a stronger scent you can add a few drops of essential oil (citrus, cinnamon, mint and/or rose.) It will be used to help with the burning of petitions before ritual begins. Florida water is a multipurpose blessing perfume and is used to cleanse space, attract favorable spirits and for blessings.

Tea leaf reading

On a note, in my work as a herbalist, focusing specifically on the unhoused population as well as those unable to afford medical care, I have found that utilizing the magic of herbs to be one of the most life changing practices you can share with other people. Hekate led me to my work with herbs and continues to give me the opportunity to help others on this path. These are some simple, magical recipes you can use in tea leaf reading, pre/post ritual and for healing. Just because they are simple, it does not mean they should be used without caution, as we are all different. One herb may affect you differently than it will for someone else. You will need:

A white candle
Pen and paper
A question
A Cup
Your choice of tea

Many different variations of divination from the sediment or the splash of liquid comes from a few different countries. Wine, coffee, and milk have all been used as part of the divinatory process. Sometimes the act of gazing deep into water will promote visions of the future or issues that need to be dealt with right now. When tea as a divinatory tool is used, there is the additional medicinal aspect of the tea (green tea having antioxidants) and herbal teas all have shown to have their health benefits. In these types of tea leaf readings, It is part divination and part spellwork.

The biggest problem in learning tea leaf reading, is that people are too rigid in their interpretation of what they see within. Sometimes you do not want to see the problem just yet, it is not something you feel ready for. Without accepting the problem, you will also not be able to accept the solution. This is very much using your intuition and feeling the energy of the message coming through the plants in the cup in relation to the person you are working with. A dog may mean a protector and guide to one person, while it may represent a fear or something that may be holding another person back. This is why it is very important to be specific in the questions and to the person you are doing the divination for.

Medicinal teas and herbs

This is your time to find the herbs relating to your question (use common sense, do your research on each herb and contraindications.) Choose the herbs that best fit your question. If you feel confused or unsure of what to do, use loose leaf green tea.

Camellia Sinensis, green tea, is a great plant to work with in issues of health and well-being, to see if you will follow a project through. Green tea is a blessing of wealth and long life. These leaves easily float to the bottom of the cup.

Here are A few tea recipes, They are medicinal in many ways, so it is important that you use your own best judgement to be certain these herbs are for you. I have listed them here for you to consider in your working, they can be more difficult to use in divinations, simply because they do not always settle to the bottom of the cup. They are listed here for you to experiment with, and they can be used for different things, which I will list alongside them.

Destination Destiny
Finding the right livelihood, a source of income that supports my joyful work.

I am all that I need, I will share my gifts with the world

By Volume:

2 pt. Ginkgo leaf *Ginkgo Biloba*; Used for circulation to the brain and to encourage dreaming.

1 pt. Papaya leaf *Carica papaya*: To help one digest their options and utilize their talents.

1 pt. Skullcap leaf *Scutellaria Lateriflora*: To relax the anxious mind.

3 pt. dried Strawberry leaf *Fragaria Vesca*: To nourish the body and remind yourself of the delicious beauty in the world.

1 pt. Passion Flower leaf *Passiflora Incarnata*: To find your passion and feel its embrace. Good for relaxation and nervous

tension.

2 pt. Elderflower *Sambucus Nigra*: The growth of the flower and allowing the sunlight to feed oneself.

1 pt. Elderberry *Sambucus Nigra*: The fruit of the flower and the work put in. Nutritious, sweet and anti-viral.

Steep one tablespoon of tea per eight ounces of hot water for 20 minutes.

By the light of Her Torches:

A tea for connection to the Goddess Hekate and Her Torchlight.

Let Hekate Guide me and Heal me

By Weight:

.25 oz Mullein (Garbled)*Verbascum Thapsus:* A herb that can help you see past the veil. Helps you breathe easier.

.10 oz White Oak Bark *Quercus Alba*: An astringent addition to a tea that offers protection.

.25 oz Comfrey Leaf *Symphytum Uplandicum*: The Great healer. To see past the boundaries that you have set for yourself. Removes them.

.10 oz Calendula (Garbled) *Calendula Officinalis* To enhance your gift of prophecy. Wound Healer.

.10 oz Witch Hazel Bark *Hamamelis Virginiana*: Connects to your emotions, what it is you need clarity on. Anti-Inflammatory.

Steep one tablespoon of tea per eight ounces of water for 20 minutes.

2nd Sight Tea:

Enhance your powers of Divination, can help with creative projects.

I am open to the messages they will enhance my power

By weight:

.10 oz Blue Vervain *Verbena hastata*: Releases rigidity, allows for relaxation.

.05 oz Mugwort *Artemisia Vulgaris*: Opens you up to different layers of existence.

.05 oz California Poppy *Eschscholzia californica*: Allows for the translation of messages.

.10 oz Angelica Root *Angelica archangelica*: Protective and helps you connect with enlightened beings.

.25 oz Chopped dried Blueberry (the ones you eat!): Help you to be strong in your focus and to communicate well.

.05 oz Eyebright Herb *Euphrasia Officinalis*: To clear out Foggy vision, and pass on messages from beyond the veil.

Steep one tablespoon of herbs per eight ounces of water for 20 minutes.

This infusion can be drunk or used to wash on the area of the forehead that is referred to as "the third eye"

Hangover Remedy

Eases twitching, headaches, gastrointestinal stress and anxiety. For when you overindulged in cakes and (particularly)ale! Also, really nice to help you sleep.

I will never drink again

Equal parts by Volume:

1 pt. Marshmallow root *Althaea officinalis*: Helps reduce inflammation in the digestive tract.

1 pt. Skullcap *Scutellaria lateriflora*: Soothes jittery nerves, calms the mind. (Might put you back to sleep.)

1 pt. Wild Lettuce *Lactuca virosa*: Eases physical pain and mental suffering.

Steep one tablespoon per eight ounces of hot water for 20

minutes. Let cool and drink.

Your cup as a sacred vessel.

Cups are tools to access the psychic portions of your mind. They trigger a reaction in you to release the vision of the future. Acquire a cup for your workings that only you use for this purpose. Good examples of cups are ones that have rounded bottoms, there are no creases inside, ideally it will have a handle at one end. I often find my favorite cups at antique stores. I appreciate sturdy old restaurant cups that travel well.

If you have any cups that have been in the family and used by family, this can also be a good choice, especially beneficial if you are asking ancestors for help in finding the solution to your problems.

There are also "tea leaf reading" cups that are made to help guide you by using markings to distinguish elements/distance/ etc. These are not necessary to your progress, but can be a fun addition to your tea ceremony and teacup collection.

Once you determine what cup you will be using, be sure to gently rinse it with salt water, hand dry it gently and let it sit in the sunlight for one hour.

Placement in a teacup

Now that you have a cup, this is the part where you look into your cup and decide some placement areas. I consider the middle of the cup to be near future, and closer to the edge of the cup to be farther off. This spirals up from the middle.

Directions and elements in the tea cup:

- East (right of handle) Air, Swords, Communications, Travel, Summer Season.
- South (at the handle) Fire, Passion, Wands, Lust, Sex, Fall season.
- West (left of handle) Water, Emotions, Cups, Love, Spring

Season.

- North (Away from Handle) Earth, Stability, Pentacles, Money, Winter Season.

Write down your own placements, or write down these. Remember to not be rigid, but do have some foundation of the placement meanings for your particular teacup.

The Divination and the process

Take pictures of each step, from dry herb to finished tea.

Now that you have decided on your question, your herbs, your cup and your placement, find a quiet and comfortable table to prepare your divinatory tea. Write down your question, place it on an altar space with a candle over it. While the candle is burning over the question (safely, you don't actually want to burn the paper) write a chant or meditation. Prepare your tea. This you can do as you think on the question. You can use this for every reading, or make a new one. A simple one is as follows:

Guides, Guides,
Ancestor Spirits,
Helpful ones,
Knowing one's,
With gratitude
Shine a light on this question

Chant this three times while the candle is burning and then meditate on it. Use one teaspoon of the herbs and place in the bottom of your dry and blessed teacup. Recite the chant and then ask the question into your teacup keeping in mind the placements. Pour water over the herbs in the cup continuing your chant.

Let the tea cool, and be sure it is covered. Once it has cooled down you can take off the cover and note what you see, take a picture and ask the question again. Much of the tea should have settled but it won't hurt you to drink little bits of herb. Drink the tea, taking in the blessings of the herbs and the magic of the spell you are working. Once you are just about finished, sip the remaining liquid out of the cup. Note if there are any areas in the cup where a majority of the plant material has settled.

Allow yourself to acknowledge what imagery comes to mind when looking into the cup and processing your question. Is there a little voice inside that is whispering an answer? Do you actually see a story coming to play? Note all of your thoughts onto a piece of paper. Go over your notes and the previous days lessons if you need to.

Project: Take pictures of your process. Note what you see in the cup. Write it down. See what happens.

Typically, herbs used are varied according to location and access. Please use your best judgement in finding herbs that work best for you. Use common sense with your herb usage.

Full moon of October

On this night of the Full Hunter Moon, we seize the opportunity to manifest abundance in our homes to prepare, once again for the cold hard depths of winter. The moon rises and appears larger, with autumnal tones reminding us of the fallen leaves that scatter about the roads and of the fruits and vegetables of our harvest. We give thanks to our ancestors, as their path co-mingles with ours during this time of the thinning veil. The Goddess Hekate is near, as the veils are thinning. With this understanding, of the fallen leaves that give nourishment to the soil, we open up our energy to release and to receive. For this moon's magical working you will focus on an ancestor of blood and/or affinity. Someone you can relate to that shares aspects of your life.

You will need:

An image or item that represents them
A candle to light for this ancestor
A tool of divination (tarot, bones, crystal orb)
A lock of your hair (or other offering)
An offering for your ancestor and Hekate
Libation for you and your ancestor
Sea salt
Incense like mugwort, sage or frankincense

Be sure to prepare for your meeting by bathing in or with sea salt. This can be a scrub with salt in the shower or a full bath in saltwater. This will help cleanse and protect you during this work. Dress in new or clean clothing of your choosing.

Prepare an altar to this ancestor using their image/or item that represents them, a candle and an offering they would like (perhaps coffee, alcohol or herbs. It is up to you and how you relate to this ancestor.) Place an offering to Hekate onto the altar with an image representing her. On the night of the full moon, open up to this ancestor by speaking out loud to them, giving them gratitude for their life's work, and asking for blessings on yours. Go into meditation, letting your mind release any thought, if something creeps in, do not allow it, just let go for a minute or two. Pour a libation for you and your ancestor and cut a lock of hair for them (if possible) Then grab your tool of divination, and ask what it is you need to do to live your best and truest life. Write down these messages, and keep them on your altar till the next full moon, you will then read the divination, and divine again if you need clarity. When you have finished writing down your divination, go into meditation once more to clear your mind. Burn incense. You can do grounding work to bring yourself back to Earth, Usually, eating something high in protein can help, have cakes and ale prepared beforehand.

Full moon working ~ Scrying and Dreamwork

Have you collected rainwater over these past few months? Have you any sacred waters from Holy Wells or other Holy Places? This is a great time to put those into use. These waters are protective and call on your higher self. You do not have to use all of it, but a few drops will do.

For this working you will need:

Holy Water
A dark flat stone like obsidian or jet
Teaspoon ground mugwort herb
Lavender essential oil
Incense or smoke
A bowl or cauldron for gazing

What is Your future? What questions do you have? First meditate on your query, and write it down, to place under your bowl. You will receive the message that will most benefit you, if you only listen.

By the light of the full moon, and the stars in the sky, cleanse your cauldron with smoke, place the stone at the bottom of your cauldron, use a few drops of your sacred water if you wish to conserve it, or fill it up to an inch above your flat stone if not. (Use distilled water to fill the rest if applicable.) Crush the mugwort between your fingers and breathe in its fragrance, thinking again of your query. Place it in your bowl, and think again of your query. Add 1-2 drops of lavender essential oil, and notice the oil and how it distributes on the surface of the water. Are any images coming forth? Any messages being triggered in your mind? Blow smoke, or incense onto the surface of the water, and notice where it goes, what it does. Again, note messages. If you are having difficulty, go back to your query and ask again.

Let the water bathe in the light of the moon overnight. You will gather and strain off the bulk materials the next day before sunrise. The water can now be used to help with your dreamwork, as the power and energy of the full moon has empowered it. Add to a spray bottle, or use a splash before going to sleep for this purpose. The energy of the water is that of the guides that protect you, the powers within you and the never-ending energy source that is the light of the moon.

Full Moon Working: Scrying, blessing and amulet work
You will need:

A small mirror
A moonstone
Rainwater
A bowl to fit them all
A clearing incense (optional)

You will need to be outside, gathering the energy of the moon's light. It does not have to be completely visible, but you will need to be in a place that the moon's light will touch. Prepare your space with incense if needed. Place your mirror at the bottom of the bowl, and pour the rainwater on top of it, this will help to amplify the energy using the reflective qualities of both water and mirror. Look into the bowl with the two in it, gather the reflection of the moon and gaze into it, allowing the moon's light to be reflected onto your face. Scry into it and give thanks to your ancestors, ask a question if you seek an answer. Place the moonstone on top of the mirror in the bowl and allow for the energy of the moon to be reflected onto the moonstone. Say out loud and into the working:

Moon and water,
Mirror and moonstone
Open my mind's eye to see;
As above and so below

The power is within me.

Take out the stone and carry it with you to inspire your own natural intuition, save the water to use as a splash, or put in a spray bottle for later use. You can add a few drops of essential oil that you find pleasing. Take the mirror and place it on your altar to gaze upon in the morning for your daily practice. (A daily blessing you give yourself every day)

Waning moon

The silver cup that holds onto quartz and tourmaline, spilling into its own fluidity. Energy that protects and directs like the arrow. This is the healing time, the time of emetic moon magic. Poison you have held onto and stored in your body and mind must come out now, it is sometimes uncomfortable, but always necessary. The blowback from the energetic extensions of your power, time to acknowledge where your suffering comes from.

Witches torch

You will need:

3 or more mullein seed stalks
2 cups beeswax
3 ml mugwort essential oil (optional)
Mason jar
Saffron threads (you can sub dandelion flower petals if saffron is unavailable)
Wax/Parchment paper
A Brush (optional)

Making torches can be a messy proposition, so be sure to cover the area with old newspapers or some kind of protective shield that you will be working on. Alternatively, you can add herbs and oils that you feel represent Hekate. Use incense to cleanse the area, and prepare your workstation with wax paper to place your finished torches on.

Mullein seed stalks are found on second year plants of your common Mullein *Verbascum Thapsus*. This is not usually something you can purchase, but it is plentiful and easy to grow. It might behoove you to go on a hike to find this plant and ask for the guidance of the Mighty Queen. Harvest the seed stalk and let it dry before use. Use your mason jar as a double boiler. Place the mason jar with beeswax into a pot of water. Melt the beeswax down stirring constantly, and when it is fully melted, turn the heat off then add the saffron and mugwort to gently mix it into the beeswax. After stirring the mix, use heat resistant gloved hands to dip the mullein stalks into the wax. (You can also Paint on the wax, if you do not have lots of it to work with.) Allow the wax to drip a bit and be somewhat dry. You will dip each stalk three times, allowing it to cool between dipping. When you are done, place the finished torches onto the wax paper to fully dry. You can save any leftover wax for another time. Typically, when I burn these torches, it is outside in a fire safe area, where I will be with the flames the whole time. Mullein is a plant that has been used to reveal secrets, and is associated with the dead.

Waxing moon

Noumenia are the first days of the lunar cycle, when you may fill your kadiskos for the Gods to bless the home. It is necessary to take in ideas and thoughts. At the beginning of the illumination time, the silver slip of night begins to show, offering a seductive gaze into our own wants and requests. Legs spread and reveal the warmth of the cave, we enter it, only to realize that the Goddess is actually within us. It is a celebration of a celebration; as we ingest the thought that every day is a Holy Day. Contemplate the following in this order on the waxing moon cycle.

- What are you grateful for?

- What are you seeking to manifest?
- How will you impact the lives of those you come into contact with?
- Who is your highest self?

Kadiskos

Prepare a mason jar or another receptacle. Place in it, offerings of olive oil, honey, water and on bay leaves, write down in a word or two what you are grateful for. Place it in a spot in your kitchen, or on your household altar. Light a candle (safely) on top of the jar, and say at least three things you are grateful for this past moon time. Remind yourself of what you wish to manifest in the next moon cycle. This jar will be refreshed every Noumenia, that is; a clean jar is replaced with new offerings and gratitude for the month. This is based off the Greek kadiskos, that would be filled with bits of food to feed the Gods.

The Flying Ointment

As Hekate is a Goddess of Witchcraft, many of her devotees become interested in the magic and medicine of Flying Ointments. Witches flying ointments have been around for centuries. We know now that our skin is the largest organ on our body, depending on physical condition and health of the skin it will absorb a percentage of what you put on it. Absorption and penetration are different. Absorption means the particles are small enough to travel into the bloodstream, while penetration is more skin deep. Beeswax and heavy oils will sit on the skins surface protecting it from the elements. Certain essential oils or alcohol (as with liniments) are absorbed into the skin much more so than, say, olive oil. You will get a different effect when using different bases as well. Each person is different and there is no percentage that can be accurate enough to apply across the board that will absorb into your skin. So, it is safe to say that flying ointments will affect everyone differently. Start slowly and proceed with respect to the animal and plant that gave its life for the ointment and with your body that you currently navigate. How much you apply over whatever surface area, what base you apply, how long it is on the skin, and the temperature (heat or hot cold therapy) will all affect absorption. Since we are talking about flying ointments, you do not necessarily want it to have maximum absorption. I do not recommend making alcohol extract or essential oil out of poisonous substances to put on the skin for example. This can be too toxic and absorb too quickly into the skin causing a bad reaction. You may get one anyway if you are sensitive or allergic to the plants.

Ancient recipes for flying ointments are vague, and are not as reliable for creating a modern version. They are fun to read, and open to interpretation but require a little more research than adding the herbs to a fat.

One of the earliest historical references to Flying ointments is from Lucius Apuleius. Golden Ass, Book III Chapter 16 (160 AD)

On a day Fotis came running to me in great fear, and said that her mistress, to work her sorceries on such as she loved, intended the night following to transform herself into a bird, and to fly whither she pleased. Wherefore she willed me privily to prepare myself to see the same. And when midnight came she led me softly into a high chamber, and bid me look through the chink of a door: where first I saw how she put off all her garments, and took out of a certain coffer sundry kinds of boxes, of the which she opened one, and tempered the ointment therein with her fingers, and then rubbed her body therewith from the sole of the foot to the crown of the head, and when she had spoken privily with herself, having the candle in her hand, she shaked parts of her body, and behold, I perceived a plume of feathers did burgen out, her nose waxed crooked and hard, her nails turned into claws, and so she became an owl. Then she cried and screeched like a bird of that kind, and willing to prove her force, moved herself from the ground by little and little, til at last she flew quite away.

In the Golden Ass, Lucious seeks to use magic to transform himself into a bird, but instead, is transformed into an ass. It is a novel, and a work of fiction, but still, one wonders where the author learned of the magic of such herbs. It is also a lesson in trial and error, he did not get the result he wanted, but instead had a less glamorous transformation than expected.

One of my favorite references to flying ointments mentions using "*soot*" and the effect of rubbing to make "*ruddy and warm*" heat and friction will increase circulation and absorption.

Giovan Battista Della Porta. From *De Miraculis Rerum Naturalium (The Wanderling)*, Book II, Chapter XXVI (1558 AD)

Lamiarum Unguenta:

Although they mix in a great deal of superstition, it is apparent nonetheless to the observer that these things can result from a natural force. I shall repeat what I have been told by them. By boiling (a certain fat) in a copper vessel, they get rid of its water, thickening what is left after boiling and remains last. Then they store it, and afterwards boil it again before use: with this, they mix celery, aconite, poplar leaves and soot. Or, in alternative: sium, acorus, cinquefoil, the blood of a bat, nightshade (Solanum) and oil; and if they mix in other substances they don't differ from these very much. Then they smear all the parts of the body, first rubbing them to make them ruddy and warm and to ratify whatever had been condensed because of cold. When the flesh is relaxed and the pores open up, they add the fat (or the oil that is substituted for it) - so that the power of the juices can penetrate further and become stronger and more active, no doubt. And so they think that they are borne through the air on a moonlit night to banquets, music, dances and the embrace of handsome young men of their choice.

While it is not a scientific approach to flying ointments, it is based on accounts from other sources. The making *"ruddy and warm"* is meant to imply that vigorous rubbing and heat will increase circulation and absorption. Heating of the fat for hours and sometimes days over a fire will take some time to reach the thick consistency you might expect from an ointment. The boiling of the fat over time to make it thick, is certainly used in topical preparations when thickeners are not as available or needed. Beeswax is often used to help make an ointment solid and consistent, also it offers the maker less time to create a balm such as this. Does it change the properties? It can certainly change the way the ointment will absorb. Beeswax tends to sit on the skin and protects the area, which can allow for a longer and slower release time.

The soot implied in the above certainly has roots in witchcraft. The char of a ritual fire will contain the energy of a bonfire on a hedonistic night, or the burned offerings of herbs to deity will certainly increase the magical power of a flying ointment. Remnants of worship and ritual in an invocative ointment dedicated to flight and the connection to the blessings of the Goddess.

The Soot
You will need:

Fine grain salt (warding)
Powdered herb of yarrow (courage)
Isopropyl alcohol 50-99%
Firesafe iron cauldron

Cleanse your cauldron with incense before use. Add equal parts of powdered yarrow and fine grain salt to the cauldron, fill to the top of the mixture with the alcohol and light it. It will burst into flames so use caution. As it is lit, say what it is you need from your working. Sit with it and chant to Hekate. It can burn for a while so prepare yourself.

Once the fire is done burning and the ash has cooled, you will break up the hardened herb mix and powder it in a mortar and pestle. This can be used in your flying ointment and has many other uses. Typically, I make a protection powder for safe travels and for the ceremonial use of flying ointments. The mix should be charred, if not as dark as desired, you can add more alcohol and herbs and start again.

Of course, any soot that is left over from a particular ritual or offering may be a good choice if it is an energy you wish to bring into your ointment.

Witches Ointment #1
There should be caution when using the ointment. If you are pregnant, nursing, under 5-foot-tall or have heart, liver or kidney

problems, do not get on this ride. Do not eat it, do not put in your eyes or in your vagina or in your rectum. This is excellent to use before ritual, during meditation and for astral travel.

A pint of leaf lard (a choice lard from the kidneys and loins of a hog)

Finger sized *Mandragora Officinarum* chopped (pruners work for this as they can be hard to cut when dry)

Handful of *Papaver Somniferum* seed (ground using mortar and pestle)

A hands length wormwood branch *Artemisia Absinthium*

Handful of poplar buds *(Populus Nigra or Populus Alba)*

A tablespoon of finely ground herb soot

Optional: beeswax to harden

Using the double boiler method - add all of the herbs, herb char, then the fat on top. Let sit on low heat all night covered. At midnight be sure to chant into it three times

Witches Flight, Clarity of Sight
Revealed in darkness by your light
For visions we Scry
Fly, Witch, Fly!
Amazon Blood Mothers flying ointment chant

Strain the roughage from the fat and if you want to add beeswax, first heat the fat and add the beeswax to it, thoroughly mixing it together. Put it in appropriately labeled containers and save for later use.

Witches Flying Ointment # 2:

Messages from the other side.

Please note, Black nightshade is toxic and can be deadly when consumed raw. Use caution when handling this plant.

1-pint olive oil

3 leaves and approx. 6 berries of black nightshade *Solanum Nigrum*

½ cup ground poppy seed *Papaver Somniferum*

1 cup dried mugwort leaf (*Artemisia Vulgaris*)

Tablespoon herb char

Mugwort essential oil (*Artemisia Vulgaris*)

Approx. ¼ cup beeswax

Using the double boiler method - add all of the herbs, herb soot, then the fat on top. Let sit on low heat all night covered. Strain and add back to the heat with beeswax till mixed and melted. Take off the heat and add 20 drops of mugwort essential oil. Then place in appropriately labeled jars.

Witches Flying Ointment #3
Dreamwork with Hekate and Somnus

    Equal parts:

    Mugwort *Artemisia Vulgaris*

    Wormwood *Artemisia Absinthium*

    Poppy seed *Papaver Somniferum*

    Optional: Essential oil of vetiver and cinnamon

    Add enough leaf lard or oil where herbs are ½ the total volume.

Using the double boiler method - add all of the herbs then the fat or oil on top. Let sit on low heat all night covered. Let cool, add the essential oils if desired.

Ways to use flying ointments
The simplest and most common way to use a flying ointment is just before sleep, when you wish to receive a message. I would recommend specificity when using it. Writing out a sentence or

two on what you need to know in a journal. Say it out loud and hold it in your thoughts. Apply the mandrake flying ointment to the back of your neck and the bottoms of your feet. Chant three times:

Witches Flight, Clarity of Sight
Revealed in darkness by your light
For visions we Scry
Fly, Witch, Fly!
Amazon Blood Mothers Flying Ointment Chant

Lay down to rest. This is best done after a hot cleansing bath.

Visit the Cemetery
Bring a tarot deck or divination tool of your choosing
Black nightshade flying ointment
An offering to the spirits (flowers, brandy etc.)
3 pennies
A question
A cleansing herb such as mugwort or wormwood

At the cemetery gates, cleanse yourself with the herb, apply the black nightshade ointment onto the back of your neck where it meets the skull and massage into the tops of your shoulders. Say this prayer:

You are death,
And once alive
As I am alive,
I will be death.
I honor our journey

State your question. Leave your 3-penny offering at the gate and enter. Walk around the cemetery till you find a space that feels welcoming. This will be based on intuition. Find a spirit you can connect with. Again, state your question and prepare your tool of divination. Lay out the cards and ask the question again. Take a picture of the cards if you need, and look at the messages. Leave your offering to the spirit and head back. You may notice tonight, that you will have dreams of the past dead. This may be pets that have passed and have a message for you, it may be a person on the other side that you know, sometimes it will be ancestors that you have never met. They all have an important message for you. Listen. Cleanse with herbs again if needed. Use to anoint a small amount onto pulse points before ritual to enhance the experience.

Hekate's Garden

From the Orphic Argonautica describing Hekate's Garden:

In the Furthest Recesses of the enclosure was a sacred Grove Shaded by Flourishing trees. In it there were many laurels and Cornels and tall plane trees. Within the grass was carpeted with low growing plants with powerful roots. Famous Asphodel, pretty maidenhair, rushes, galangal, delicate verbena, sage, Hedge mustard, purple honeysuckle, healing cassidony, Flourishing field basil, mandrake, hulwort, in addition to fluffy Dittany, fragrant saffron, nose-smart, there too lion-foot, greenbrier, chamomile, black poppy, alcua, all-heal, white hellebore, aconite, and many other noxious plants grew from the earth. In the middle of a stout oak tree with heaven high trunk spread its branches Out over much of the grove. On it hung, spread out over a long branch, the golden fleece, Over which watched a terrible snake.

Herbs used in the Temple of the Bones will be herbs that you can find locally, and are not always mentioned in historical reference to her. Hekate's Pharmacopeia extends to all magical herbs within the Temple and all herbs have magic within them. Here are some specific energies of the plants most commonly used in The Temple of the Bones. Look at the specific Latin names here, sometimes substitutions are made, but they do not always have the same effect. For instance, due to the fact that mandrake can take a year to germinate, oftentimes May apple is substituted and is even called mandrake in some places. May apple is much easier to obtain, but is in a different family of plants. Due to the rarity of mandragora officinarum, the cost of obtaining a root can be prohibitive. It may be best to try your hand at growing a few in your own garden.

Mandragora officinarum ~ **Mandrake**
Mandrake has been used as a plant of fertility and as an aphrodisiac. In flying ointments, it was made notorious during the witch hunts, when it was believed to grow out of earth that had been fed with the urine and semen of a hanged man.

Papaver Somniferum ~ **Poppy**
Named after Somnus the Roman God of sleep. The poppy can help relax and soothe one into slumber, it is also symbolic of the long sleep of death and the fecundity that comes from well-nourished earth. The poppy reproduces with its seed, and it produces a lot of it, as it is of death, so it is of life and fertility.

Artemisia Absinthium ~ **Wormwood**
Thought to be named after the Goddess Artemis, one who is often conflated with Hekate, wormwood is a protective and warming plant that can help ease you to the places where you need to travel. It can help to open up the past, and offers protection on your journey. Sometimes this is about contemplating your dark side, shedding light on those things that can be harder to process. Please note that due to the thujone content, wormwood should be burned with proper ventilation or outside only.

Artemisia Vulgaris ~ **Mugwort**
Mugwort is used to help access and recall dreams. Oftentimes it is used in balms and ritual oil to help with divination. Bundles of it are burned to purify space and offer protection, mugwort bundles are hung over the bed to encourage dreaming.

Populus Nigra ~ **Black Poplar**
Black poplar is high in salicin which is where we get our modern-day aspirin. As such, it is anti-inflammatory and can soothe aches and pains. It is used magically in folk magic to ease heartache and suffering. It is a herb of divination and ancestral connection.

Solanum Nigrum ~ Black Nightshade

A feral garden plant that can be found in liminal places, waste sites and on the borders of your gardens. A plant that represents the dark of the moon (to some, Saturn), and a herb of Hekate. This herb is best used when seeking to contact the dead and receive messages from them. Use topically and apply to tools specific to death and ancestors.

Vetiveria zizanioides ~ Vetiver

Vetiver is used to provide protection and promote feelings of calm. It has a deep earthy scent, so it makes a pleasant balm for relaxing the mind and body. This can be exceptionally grounding, if you need an anchor to the Earth during astral travel or aspecting work.

Genus Cinnamomum ~ Cinnamon

Warming and stimulating allowing for better circulation. Cinnamon draws on the energy of the phoenix, and will help you to rise up from the ashes.

Achillea Millefolium ~ Yarrow

Yarrow is useful for divination and astral travel. It is well known for its protective qualities as it was named after Achilles, likely due to the fact that yarrow can stop blood. Protection is important during sleep and astral travel; these are times when you are more vulnerable to spiritual and psychic attack.

Ruta Graveolens ~ Rue

Rue is a strongly scented herb that is traditionally used for warding off the evil eye, and to offer protection from curses or the jealousy of others. It is best gathered at night, the volatile oils in the plant can cause skin irritation when exposed to sunlight.

Temple of the Bones Ritual Pit

The following outlines are from a few of the Temple of the Bones open to the public rituals in Oakland, California. These outlines can be edited but a few things remain the same, It is a ritual to Hekate, petitions are released, Heaven, Earth and sea are called on as her "Planes of Power", the ancestors are honored as listed and there is a divination with bones at the end. There is a bit of a difference in what can be done feasibly in a public ritual versus one with coven members that you work with consistently, all of the following rituals have been open to the public, created and led by The Temple of the Bones witches.

In the Temple of the Bones there are no Priest/x/ess, though Bird and Briar of the original Temple both had training in different covens and traditions and are High Priest/x/ess and/or initiates of those traditions. For the sake of The Temple of the Bones, all attendees are witches and those who have the responsibility of an activity in ritual are loosely called Head Witch or Lead Witch. Each witch in charge of an activity is responsible for all that they say and do within the circle. Most witches in a lead position have some experience working in public ritual already, though this is not the case for all and it has been a loose training ground for solitary witches to put their feet to the fire. If a portion of the ritual is blank, then these are parts that were not meant to be shared or repeated by others, but are meant to be filled in from your own perspective, allowing you to access the energy of Hekate, rather than read from this guide. As hard as we try to not establish a hierarchy, there is no doubt that experience and loyalty should be held in high regard. With that said, a lion does not need to tell you it is a lion, and all should have the awareness to see who has done, and continues to do, the work within the Temple.

Temple of the Bones Hekate Enodia; She of the Path

((−)) means a role needs to be filled

Set up: Altar should be set up on an appropriate altar cloth with a representation of Hekate (statue, picture or other item) the bones in a small cauldron, a larger cauldron for the Planes of Power invocation, water, incense, and herbs to be used in ritual, a basket of tea lights and one candle for the Goddess Hekate and another for the elevated ancestor. Petitions are at the ready in a cauldron. Two lighters or matches, one for petitions and one for the ancestor portion. There should be enough open and fire safe space to place all of the ancestors' tealights at the appropriate time, sometimes a large plate or serving tray helps, as wax does tend to spill onto the altar cloth. All items for the ritual workings need to be procured. Take note of what it is you will need for this ritual.

Welcome: ((−)) Welcome attendees to temple, introduce Hekate as a many-faced goddess, tonight we will put the oil made last month to use for blessings and protection in the new year. Talk about Hekate Enodia, She of the Path. Explain historical and modern variations of Hekate. Make sure everyone has their cell phones off or on silent, explain where the bathrooms are. Tonight, we will be blessing the new statue. Talk about the herbs: mugwort, wormwood, rue, peppermint, dandelion and why we are using them.

((−)) Petitions: Process outside to burn petitions with drum or rattle and low humming. Florida Water to help ignite the flames in the cauldron ~ Whispered wishes for Hekate to acknowledge and bless the petitions. Lights dimmed. ((−)) will drum heartbeat.

((−)) Cleansing: When entering through the doors each person is cleansed with fresh wormwood or other appropriate herb. Each

attendee will also take from a bowl a tealight for the ancestors to be used later.

((−)) Circle Cast: with blade.

((−)) Planes of Power: After creating sacred space in the circle casting, we will invoke Hekate's three planes of power/realms: land (herbs), sea (water), and sky (incense). Starting with her highest realm, air, we will smoke the bowl/basin with sage or incense, we will add herbs for Earth and finally oil or water to represent waters and sea. By uniting her three planes of power we invoke her powers of divination (air), mastery of magical herbs (earth), and keeper of mysteries (water). We will be using this oil or water in the working that follows.

((−)) Ancestor invocations: The person leading this portion calls in one elevated ancestor and lights a central white candle on the altar table; they then direct the others to go up one by one to light their tea light from the candle flame and place upon the altar while calling in an ancestor silently or out loud.

((−)): Invoking the Goddess Hekate Enodia

> *I call Einodian Hekate, lovely dame,*
> *Of earthly, watery and celestial frame,*
> *Sepulchral, in a Saffron Veil array'd,*
> *Leas'd with dark ghosts that wander thro' the shade;*
> *Persian, unconquerable huntress hail!*
> *The world's key bearer never doomed to fail;*
> *On the rough rock to wander thee delights,*
> *Leader and nurse be present in our rites*
> *Propitious grant our just desires success,*
> *Accept our homage, and the incense bless.*
> (Translation by Thomas Taylor) from the Chaldean Oracles

Witches are invited to give offerings at the altar of Hekate Enodia. A bottle of wine and head of garlic can be set on the altar for those who do not bring an offering, so all may participate. Can be poured into a cup or set on a plate set aside for Hekate.

((−)) *The Working:* Blessing the oil by Lead Witch with group effort. Explain each herb and their properties, why we are using them in this oil. Teaching the chant. Blessing the statue, Blessing of the attendees.

Each attendee dips their hand in the bowl of blessed oil, anoints the statue and calls on one aspect of Hekate with a *"hail and welcome"*, then Head Witch will bless their boots. There will be a throne where each person is veiled, their path (and boots) blessed and then the veil is lifted.

> *Triple way, path revealed;*
> *Dancing in darkness, you heal;*
> *Let us walk now, the way;*
> *Hekate, Hekate Hekate*

((−)) **Divination:** The person leading this section explains that bones and other natural curios are powerful sources of energy and have unique meanings which apply to our lives. Then one by one, those in attendance come, draw a bone, are told which bone it is, place the bone on the altar and are sent back to contemplate its meaning in their message.

Gratitude to Hekate and Hail and Farewell: Give gratitude to the Mighty Queen using her name and epithet, and Head Witch gives a *"Hail and Farewell"*.

Hail and Farewell Ancestors: Give gratitude to all the ancestors, and a *"Hail and Farewell"* (candles may be extinguished now, and attendees may take them home, or these will be placed on the ancestor altar to be burned at a later time. They are extinguished now, so the wax has time to cool)

Release Planes of Power: *"We release these elements of Hekate of Heaven, Earth and Sea, we are grateful for their lessons and their gifts, Blessings to all! So Mote it be! Hail and Farewell!"*

Opening the Circle: By blade

Collection of offerings to pay rent on the space or purchase supplies as needed.

Cakes and Ale; Socialization.

What Items might you need for this ritual? What preparations in advance need to happen before ritual can begin?

Temple of Bones Hekate Amibousa; She Who Transforms

((−)) means a role needs to be filled

Set up: Altar should be set up on an appropriate altar cloth with a representation of Hekate (statue, picture or other item) the bones in a small cauldron, a larger cauldron for the Planes of Power invocation, water, incense, and herbs to be used in ritual, a basket of tea lights and one candle for the Goddess Hekate and another for the elevated ancestor. Petitions are at the ready in a cauldron. Two lighters or matches, one for petitions and one for the ancestor portion. There should be enough open and fire safe space to place all of the ancestors' tealights at the appropriate time, sometimes a large plate or serving tray helps, as wax does tend to spill onto the altar cloth. All items for the ritual workings need to be procured. Take note of what it is you will need for this ritual.

Welcome attendees to the Temple of the Bones, introducing Hekate as a many-faced goddess. Tonight, we will work with her facet as Hekate Amibousa, or She Who Transforms. While

Hekate has many different epithets, this one hails from a triangular bronze plaque depicting three images of Hekate found at the Pergamon Altar in the ancient Greek City of Pergamon. At the foot of each of her images is inscribed a different name: Dione, Phoibe, and Nychie, meaning "Goddess", "Bright", and "Nocturnal One," respectively. Amibousa lifts her divine torches in the darkness to guide us on our paths. The fire of her torches is the fire of transformation. Tonight, we offer her ourselves for her to bewitch with her power and magic. Tonight, we let her transform us.

((−)) Petitions: Process outside to burn petitions with drum or rattle and low humming. Florida Water to help ignite the flames in the cauldron Whispered wishes for dreams to come true in all the petitions. Lights dimmed. **((−))** will drum heartbeat.

((−)) Cleansing: When entering through the doors each person is cleansed with fresh rue or other appropriate herb. Each attendee will also take from a bowl a tealight for the ancestors to be used later.

((−)) Circle Cast with Garlic: Cast a circle around the workspace using the head of garlic. Each person can take a clove of garlic off the head and hold on to it to give as an offering to Hekate later after she is invoked into the space. Move deosil, in a clockwise motion, saying,

We are protected, within this circle

((−)) Planes of Power: After creating sacred space in the circle casting, we will invoke Hekate's three planes of power/realms, so that we are not just creating sacred space but creating her sacred space: land (herbs), sea (water), and sky (incense). Starting with her highest realm, air, we will smoke the bowl/basin with sage or incense, we will add herbs for Earth and finally water for sea. By uniting her three planes of power we invoke her powers of divination (air), mastery of magical herbs (earth), and keeper of mysteries (water).

((−)) *Ancestor invocations:* The person leading this portion calls in one elevated ancestor and lights a central white candle on the altar table; they then direct the others to go up one by one to light their tea light from the candle flame and place upon the altar while calling in an ancestor silently or out loud.

((−)): *Invoking the Goddess Hekate:* We begin by making an offering to our goddess. Tonight's offering will consist of incense, wine and a bulb of garlic into the center of which burns a black candle anointed with oil. Once the offering is made, she will be invoked using Hymn VI to Hekate by Proclus.

Hymn VI: To Hekate
(Trans: E. Vogt, 1957)

Hail, many-named Mother of the Gods, whose children are bright
Hail, mighty Hekate of the Threshold
Shape the course of my life with luminous Light
And make it laden with good things,
Drive sickness and evil from my limbs.
And when my soul rages about worldly things,
Deliver me purified by your soul-stirring rituals.
Yes, give me your hand I pray
And reveal to me the pathways of divine guidance that I long for,
Then shall I gaze upon that precious Light
Whence I can flee the evil of our dark origin.
Yes, give me your hand I pray,
And when I am weary bring me to the haven of piety with your winds.
Hail, many-named mother of the Gods, whose children are bright

Hail, mighty Hekate of the Threshold

((−)) The Working: Tonight, we are working with Hekate Amibousa, She Who Transforms, to help transform us into more powerful witches. Everyone will receive a nail, a black 6in candle, a matchbook, and a printed copy of her bronze tablet from the Pergamon Altar. The tablet shows three images of Hekate, each of which have "Amibousa" written at their feet. At their heads they all have a unique name inscribed: Dione, Phoibe, and Nychie meaning "Goddess," "Bright," and "Nocturnal One." This ancient Greek tablet shows Hekate as a goddess of illumination and of night time. A goddess whose powerful torches can create transformation. Tonight, we call on Hekate Amibousa to transform us with her torches into witches of greater power, skill, and understanding.

Making the torches: We will begin by calling her names gently out loud as we carve them into the candles. Next, we will bind the candles to our own energy by anointing them with our own spit. For the final part of the ritual, participants will be guided to seek out some personal space where they can set the tablet and candle on a flat surface. On our own, we will place the candles on the black circle in the center of the tablet, perform a small, personal prayer to Hekate, and then light the candle. We will all take a moment to sit silently in the light of the candle flames, Hekate's torches, and feel her power begin to transform us magically. After 99 seconds the candles will be extinguished and we will return to our seats.

The candles and tablets can then be taken home for further use over the course of this next moon. In a dark room with no other light, make your call to her, light the candle, and bathe in its illumination as you allow Hekate to transform you into a creature of greater power, wisdom, and magic. Each time you do this you allow her to widen the current of magical energy that runs through you. Finish burning by the next new moon, and dispose of any remains at a crossroads.

((−)) Divination: The person leading this section explains that bones and other natural curios are powerful sources of energy and have unique meanings which apply to our lives. They inform everyone that at the bottom of the ritual outline there is a short list of interpretations for each bone in the set. Then one by one those in attendance come, draw a bone, are told which bone it is, replace the bone, and are sent back to contemplate its meaning in their life.

Gratitude to Hekate and Hail and Farewell: ((−))
Hymn VI: To Hekate
  Proclus Diadochus (Trans: E. Vogt, 1957)

Hail, many-named Mother of the Gods, whose children are bright
Hail, mighty Hekate of the Threshold
Shape the course of my life with luminous Light
And make it laden with good things,
Drive sickness and evil from my limbs.
And when my soul rages about worldly things,
Deliver me purified by your soul-stirring rituals.
Yes, give me your hand I pray
And reveal to me the pathways of divine guidance that I long for,
Then shall I gaze upon that precious Light
Whence I can flee the evil of our dark origin.
Yes, give me your hand I pray,
And when I am weary bring me to the haven of piety with your winds.
Hail, many-named mother of the Gods, whose children are bright
Hail, mighty Hekate of the Threshold
HAIL and Farewell

Hail and Farewell Ancestors: ((—)) Give gratitude to all the ancestors, and a *"Hail and Farewell"* (candles may be extinguished now, and attendees may take them home, or these will be placed on the ancestor altar to be burned at a later time. They are extinguished now, so the wax has time to cool.)

Planes of Power ((—)) *"We release these elements of Hekate of Heaven, Earth and Sea, we are grateful for their lessons and their gifts, Blessings to all! So Mote it be! Hail and Farewell!"*

Opening the Circle: ((—)) In a counterclockwise motion, the Lead Witch who cast the circle, opens the circle. Collection of monetary offerings to pay for the space and cakes and ale.

Temple of the Bones Hekate Apotropaia; She Who Averts
((—)) means a role needs to be filled

Set up: Altar should be set up on an appropriate altar cloth with a representation of Hekate (statue, picture or other item) the bones in a small cauldron, a larger cauldron for the Planes of Power invocation, water, incense, and herbs to be used in ritual, a basket of tea lights and one candle for the Goddess Hekate and another for the elevated ancestor. Petitions are at the ready in a cauldron. Two lighters or matches, one for petitions and one for the ancestor portion. There should be enough open and fire safe space to place all of the ancestors' tealights at the appropriate time, sometimes a large plate or serving tray helps, as wax does tend to spill onto the altar cloth. All items for the ritual workings need to be procured. Take note of what it is you will need for this ritual.

((—)) **Petitions:** Process outside to burn petitions with drum or rattle and low humming. Florida Water to help ignite the flames in the cauldron Whispered wishes for dreams to come true in all the petitions. Lights dimmed. ((−)) will drum heartbeat.

((−)) *Cleansing:* When entering through the doors each person is cleansed with fresh rue or other appropriate herb. Each attendee will also take from a bowl a tealight for the ancestors to be used later.

((−)) *Circle Cast:* Passing of the skull, we are all connected, we will all one day meet death, we hope to greet it as a friend... Each person looks into the skull as it is passed around the circle. Introduction of changes: Death is inevitable, change is inevitable, our planet is a Temple of Bones, in this place we experience the vision of the world. As holders of the key we unlock the doorway to our path on the crossroads in times of chaos. As torchbearers, It is up to us to carry on the fires from the embers of destruction to light the path and see the way. Like the snake, we shed our skin and become new again.

((−)) *Directions:* Call in directions/cast sacred space through use of her three realms, land (herbs), sea (water), and sky (incense). Smoke the cauldron with incense, add the herbs, and then add the water. At the end each person can take home some of the water that has been blessed on the altar of Hekate.

((−)) *Ancestor invocations:* The person leading this portion calls in one elevated ancestor and lights a central white candle on the altar table; they then direct the others to go up one by one to light their tea light from the candle flame and place upon the altar while calling in an ancestor silently or out loud.

((−)) *Calling in Hekate:* Head Witch leads in the Invocation of Hekate Apotropaia.

Hekate Apotropaia She who averts!
Protect us with your mighty power!
Queen of the Crossroads, Shining One,
Guide us out of misery, be with us this hour!
Help us release this suffering and pain,
And that in never visits again!

The Lead Witch who did the Invocation of Hekate gives her offerings and instructs all to do so if they feel called. (Wine, garlic, and anything attendees have brought, should be placed at the altar.)

*((−)) **The Working:*** Offer a Prayer to Hekate, *"Hekate Apotropaia I ask of you, Transform any curses, evil and hatred that have been sent to me into energy I can use for my benefit, and anything that cannot be transformed be sent to the Earth to be recycled."*
Creating little bags to bind the shit that they need to be rid of, to free themselves... to be taken away and destroyed, to be transformed, all that cannot be transformed be returned to the earth to be recycled. left at the crossroads on their own time. Fill with their regret, anger, jealousy, hurt, rage.
Fill with thorns, pieces of charcoal, stones, snake skin, all symbolic of the things we need to be rid of. To be buried on their own time someplace at a crossroad to be transformed. Music playing as needed.

*((−)) **Divination:*** The witch leading this section explains that bones and other natural curios are powerful sources of energy and have unique meanings which apply to our lives. Then one by one those in attendance come, draw a bone, are told which bone it is, replace the bone, and are sent back to contemplate its meaning in their life.

*((−)) **Gratitude to Hekate and Hail and Farewell:***

*((−)) **Hail and Farewell Ancestors:*** Give Gratitude to all the ancestors, and a *"Hail and Farewell"* (candles may be extinguished now, and attendees may take them home, or these will be placed on the ancestor altar to be burned at a later time. They are extinguished now, so the wax has time to cool.)

*((−)) **Planes of Power***

> *"We release these elements of Hekate of Heaven, Earth and Sea, we are grateful for their lessons and their gifts, Blessings to all! So Mote it be! Hail and Farewell!"*

*((−)) **Opening the Circle:***

*((−)) **Collection of offerings and cakes and ale.***

Temple of Bones Hekate Astrodia:
Who walks the Stars

((−)) means a role needs to be filled

Set up: Altar should be set up on an appropriate altar cloth with a representation of Hekate (statue, picture or other item) the bones in a small cauldron, a larger cauldron for the Planes of Power invocation, water, incense, and herbs to be used in ritual, a basket of tea lights and one candle for the Goddess Hekate and another for the elevated ancestor. Petitions are at the ready in a cauldron. Two lighters or matches, one for petitions and one for the ancestor portion. There should be enough open and fire safe space to place all of the ancestors' tealights at the appropriate time, sometimes a large plate or serving tray helps, as wax does tend to spill onto the altar cloth. All Items for the ritual workings need to be procured. Take note of what it is you will need for this ritual.

Welcome attendees to temple, introduce Hekate as a many-faced goddess, tonight we will work with her facet as Hekate

Astrodia - she who walks among the stars and holds the Dead. This ritual was performed after Sunsmith passed into the realm of ancestors, he was a Dedicant of Hekate and a regular and active attendee and witch of the Temple of the Bones.

((−)) Petitions: Process outside to burn petitions with drum or rattle and low humming. Florida Water to help ignite the flames in the cauldron Whispered wishes for dreams to come true in all the petitions. Lights dimmed. *((−))* will rattle or drum.

((−)) Cleansing: When entering through the doors each person is cleansed with fresh rue or other appropriate herb. Each attendee will also take from a bowl a tealight for the ancestors to be used later. Offer witches flying ointment to apply at the door.

((−)) Circle Cast: By blade.

((−)) Planes of Power: After creating sacred space in the circle casting, we will invoke Hekate's three planes of power/realms, so that we are not just creating sacred space but creating her sacred space: land (herbs), sea (water), and sky (incense). Starting with her highest realm, air, we will smoke the bowl/basin with sage or incense, we will add herbs for Earth and finally water for sea. By uniting her three planes of power we invoke her powers of divination (air), mastery of magical herbs (Earth), and keeper of mysteries (water).

((−)) Ancestor invocations: The person leading this portion calls in one elevated ancestor and lights a central white candle on the altar table; they then direct the others to go up one by one to light their tea light from the candle flame and place upon the altar while calling in an ancestor silently or out loud. Call in Sunsmith as the ancestor. All speak his name and speak fondly of him.

((−)) *Calling In the Goddess Hekate Astrodia:*

Mighty Hekate Astrodia of the shooting star and stardust,
We call to you with Admiration,
You of the shining light in the dark night,
With glowing heart and radiant mind
Hold our Brother, within your embrace,
Guide him by the light of your torches.
As he is, we will one day be

A moment of silence. The Lead Witch who did the Invocation of Hekate gives her offerings and instructs all to do so if they feel called. (Wine, garlic, and anything attendees have brought, should be placed at the altar.)

((−)) *Divination:* The person leading this section explains that bones and other natural curios are powerful sources of energy and have unique meanings which apply to our lives. They inform everyone that at the bottom of the ritual outline there is a short list of interpretations for each bone in the set. Then one by one those in attendance come, draw a bone, are told which bone it is, replace the bone, and are sent back to contemplate its meaning in their life.

((−)) *Gratitude to Hekate and Hail and Farewell:*

Hekate Astrodia, your grace and power are felt by all,
You shine in a flash and then you are gone,
We give you gratitude and thanks for joining us in this circle.
Hail and Farewell Hekate Astrodia.

Hail and Farewell Ancestors: ((−)) Give gratitude to all the ancestors, and a *"Hail and Farewell"* (candles may be extinguished now, and attendees may take them home, or these will be placed on the ancestor altar to be burned at a later time. They are extinguished now, so the wax has time to cool.)

((−)) *Planes of Power*

> *"We release these elements of Hekate of Heaven, Earth and Sea, we are grateful for their lessons and their gifts, Blessings to all! So Mote it be! Hail and Farewell!"*

Opening the Circle: ((−))

Collection of offerings, passing out sign in contact sheet, and cakes and ale.

Temple of Bones Anassa Eneroi; Queen of the Dead
((−)) means a role needs to be filled

Set up: Altar should be set up on an appropriate altar cloth with a representation of Hekate (statue, picture or other item) the bones in a small cauldron, a larger cauldron for the Planes of Power invocation, water, incense, and herbs to be used in ritual, a basket of tea lights and one candle for the Goddess Hekate and another for the elevated ancestor. Petitions are at the ready in a cauldron. Two lighters or matches ready, one for petitions and one for the ancestor portion of ritual. There should be enough open and fire safe space to place all of the ancestors' tealights at the appropriate time, sometimes a large plate or serving tray helps, as wax does tend to spill onto the altar cloth. All items for the ritual workings need to be procured. Take note of what it is you will need for this ritual.

Welcome attendees to the temple, introducing Hekate as a many-faced goddess, tonight we will work with her facet as Hekate Anassa Eneroi, the Queen of the Dead. Tonight, we will perform a neo-traditional Deipnon, which is an ancient ritual that was performed in virtually all Athenian households on the dark of the moon. Hekate's Deipnon, at its most basic, is a meal served to the Titan Hekate and the restless dead once a lunar month. Ancient Athenians believed that once a lunar month, on the dark of the moon, Hekate led the spirits of the unavenged or wrongfully killed accompanied by hounds from the underworld up from Hades. The Deipnon is performed in order to appease the restless dead as well as to cleanse the household and all who dwell there.

((−)) *Petitions:* Process outside to burn petitions with drumbeat. ((−)) will drum heartbeat.

((−)) *Cleansing:* When entering through the doors each person is cleansed with _____. Each attendee will also take from a bowl a tealight for the ancestors to be used later.

((−)) *Circle Cast:* Passing of the skull, We are all connected, We will all one day meet death... Each person looks into the skull as it is passed around the circle. Introduction of changes: Death is inevitable, change is inevitable, our planet is a Temple of Bones, in this place we experience the vision of the world. As holders of the key we unlock the doorway to our path on the crossroads in times of chaos. As torchbearers, It is up to us to carry on the fires from the embers of destruction to light the path and see the way. Like the snake, we shed our skin and become new again.

((−)) *Planes of Power:* After creating sacred space in the circle casting, we will invoke Hekate's three planes of power/realms: land (herbs), sea (water), and sky (incense). Starting with her highest realm, air, we will smoke the bowl/basin with sage or incense, we will add herbs for Earth and finally oil or water to represent waters and sea. By uniting her three planes of power we invoke her powers of divination (air), mastery of magical herbs (earth), and keeper of mysteries (water). We will be using this oil or water in the working that follows.

((−)) Ancestor invocations: The person leading this portion calls in one elevated ancestor and lights a central white candle on the altar table; they then direct the others to go up one by one to light their tea light from the candle flame and place upon the altar while calling in an ancestor silently or out loud.

((−)): Invoking the Goddess Hekate: All close their eyes. In our inner darkness, we gaze upon the doors to the Underworld slowly opening. Loud, barking snarls make their way through the muggy air as three dogs emerge from the doorway, drawing a chariot behind them. Upon this chariot stands Hekate Anassa Eneroi, Queen of the Dead. She raises a whip and her hounds' race forward. She is followed by a thousand thousand chariots of restless dead, pulled by a thousand thousand hounds. As they race their way up from the Underworld towards the moonless sky, we call to them:

> Hail, Hekate Anassa Eneroi! Hail, Queen of Night Wandering Souls! Hail, and welcome!

The Lead Witch who did the Invocation of Hekate gives her offerings and instructs all to do so if they feel called. (Wine, garlic, and anything attendees have brought, should be placed at the altar.)

((−)) Hekate's Deipnon: A Feast for the Restless Dead
((−)) means a role needs to be filled

The Deipnon is performed for three reasons: to honor Hekate, to appease the restless dead, and to purify the household and those who dwell there. It consists of three main parts: the purification of the home, the offerings of atonement, and the feast for the spirits. In this ritual we are going to perform a neo-traditional

Deipnon by observing and fulfilling all of these functions.

We will start by purifying the space so that we can move into the new month freely. This is done by cleaning the altars and fumigating the rooms with incense. Since we are working with the Greek Pantheon, we will break into groups and take five minutes to clean the altars of Hekate, Dionysus, Hermes, and Aphrodite. Once this has been completed, we will smoke the space with incense from back to front.

Next, comes the feast for the restless dead. Traditional offerings for the feast included eggs, cakes, garlic, honey, and wine. This portion will involve walking outside, to a labyrinth. There is one near the Raven's Wing at Lake Merritt, hidden in the grass between the picnic tables, but you can search, or create your own labyrinth for this portion. Everyone will bring an egg offering to the labyrinth to present to Hekate and the spirits of the dead. On the main altar there will be eggs with names of the wrongfully killed upon them. Everyone is to take one egg to process to the labyrinth and present as part of the feast. One by one, we will walk the labyrinth and present our offerings in the center as we call out the names of the restless dead written on our eggs. When these are done the offerings for Hekate will be processed last. Upon serving the meal, we will turn and walk away without looking back.

Finally comes the expiation, or the offering of atonement. In ancient times, Athenians would bring a dog into the home and allow every member of the family to touch it before it would be ritually slaughtered. As the family members placed their hands upon the dog they would transfer curses, sins, or harmful energy from themselves to the animal. Today, we have adapted this portion. Instead of sacrificing a dog, we will be taking up collections to donate to a local dog rescue foundation in honor of Hekate. There will be a cauldron by the door. If you would like to participate in the expiation by donating; you may place your offering in the cauldron.

((−)) Divination: The person leading this section explains the premises of bone divination and informs everyone that there is a short list provided of interpretations for the bones. Then one by one those in attendance come, draw a bone, are told which bone it is, replace the bone, and are sent back to contemplate its meaning in their life.

((−)) Drums

Gratitude to Hekate and Hail and Farewell: ((−))

Hail and Farewell Ancestors: **((−))** Give gratitude to all the ancestors, and a *"Hail and Farewell"* (candles may be extinguished now, and attendees may take them home, or these will be placed on the ancestor altar to be burned at a later time. They are extinguished now, so the wax has time to cool.)

((−)) Planes of Power

> *"We release these elements of Hekate of Heaven, Earth and Sea, we are grateful for their lessons and their gifts, Blessings to all! So Mote it be! Hail and Farewell!"*

Opening the Circle: ((−))

Collection of offerings, passing out sign in contact sheet, and cakes and ale.

Temple of Bones Hekate Brimo; The Angry One
((−)) means a role needs to be filled

Set up: Altar should be set up on an appropriate altar cloth with a representation of Hekate (statue, picture or other item) the bones in a small cauldron, a larger cauldron for the Planes of Power invocation, water, incense, and herbs to be used in ritual, a basket of tea lights and one candle for the Goddess Hekate and another for the elevated ancestor. Petitions are at the ready in a cauldron. Two lighters or matches, one for petitions and one for the ancestor portion. There should be enough open and fire safe space to place all of the ancestors' tealights at the appropriate time, sometimes a large plate or serving tray helps, as wax does tend to spill onto the altar cloth. All items for the ritual workings need to be procured. *Attendees were asked to take a walk this past moon cycle, and on this journey be on the lookout for an item that can be added to the Temple of Bones Bone Set. This can be a stone, bone or rock, or even something they already have that asks to be in the Temple Bone Set.* Take note of what it is you will need for this ritual.

Welcome attendees to the temple, introducing Hekate as a many-faced goddess, tonight we will work with her facet as Hekate Brimo, the Roaring Goddess. Our Anger is a gift when used in righteous ways. What has been boiling under your skin? What needs to be released to allow for your hands to work for change? Tonight, we will rage and cry, and feel victory in our hands and on our lips!

((−)) Petitions: Process outside to burn petitions with drum or rattle and low humming. Florida Water to help ignite the flames in the cauldron Whispered wishes for dreams to come true in all the petitions. Lights dimmed. **((−))** will drum heartbeat.

((−)) Cleansing: When entering through the doors each person is cleansed with fresh rue or other appropriate herb. Each attendee will also take from a bowl a tealight for the ancestors to be used later.

((−)) Circle Cast: Passing of the skull, We are all connected, We will all one day meet death. Each person looks into the skull as it is passed around the circle. Introduction of changes: Death is inevitable, change is inevitable, our planet is a Temple of Bones,

in this place we experience the vision of the world. As holders of the key we unlock the doorway to our path on the crossroads in times of chaos. As torchbearers, It is up to us to carry on the fires from the embers of destruction to light the path and see the way. Like the snake, we shed our skin and become new again.

((−)) Planes of Power: After creating sacred space in the circle casting, we will invoke Hekate's three planes of power/realms, so that we are not just creating sacred space but creating her sacred space: land (herbs), sea (water), and sky (incense). Starting with her highest realm, air, we will smoke the bowl/basin with sage or incense, we will add herbs for Earth and finally water for sea. By uniting her three planes of power we invoke her powers of divination (Air), mastery of magical herbs (Land), and keeper of mysteries (Sea).

((−)) Ancestor invocations: The person leading this portion calls in one elevated ancestor and lights a central white candle on the altar table; they then direct the others to go up one by one to light their tea light from the candle flame and place upon the altar while calling in an ancestor silently or out loud.

((−)): Invoking the Goddess Hekate: offer an invocation culminating in all attendees roaring with rage.

The Lead Witch who did the Invocation of Hekate gives her offerings and instructs all to do so if they feel called. (Wine, garlic, and anything attendees have brought, should be placed at the altar.)

((−)) The Working:

Begin the Chant low, and gradually get louder. Instruct all to follow your lead:

We call to the Queen of the Night;

To join us in our Fight!
Roaring Bitch & Righteous Witch
Guide us by your light!

We offer our blood to Hekate (Symbolic) to prepare a blood potion (made of beet juice, saffron and mugwort extract). One by one each person will come up to the cauldron and gaze in. They will tell the cauldron what makes them most angry (out loud is best but silent will work), what they need help with. They will roar. Then they receive blood from the witch on their hands, the Lead Witch paints this on their hands using a paintbrush "Blood Of Creation" then they take it to their lips "Blood of Life", then they offer it to Hekate Brimo "Blood of Death" for protection from their enemies while in battle. *"I ask for Protection from those who seek to harm me"*

((−)) gives each person a gemstone to help protect and guide. Black tourmaline, obsidian, or tiger eye are good choices as their energy is protective in nature, in addition to being blessed on the altar of Hekate

*((−)) **Divination:** Attendees were asked to take a walk this past moon cycle, and on this journey be on the lookout for an item that can be added to the Temple of Bones Bone Set. This can be a stone, bone or rock, or even something they already have that asks to be in the Temple Bone Set.* (Activity here) Each person adds their Divination Piece to the set with explanation on where it was found, and writes it down. They give it to the temple and anoint it with Hekate oil. Place in the Bone Cauldron.

Divinations begin. The person leading this section explains that bones and other natural curios are powerful sources of energy and have unique meanings which apply to our lives. They inform everyone that at the bottom of the ritual outline there is a short list of interpretations for each bone in the set. Then one by one those in attendance come, draw a bone, are told which bone it is, replace the bone, and are sent back to contemplate its meaning in their life.

((−)) Gratitude to Hekate and Hail and Farewell:

((−)) Hail and Farewell Ancestors: Give Gratitude to all the ancestors, and a *"Hail and Farewell"* (candles may be extinguished now, and attendees may take them home, or these will be placed on the ancestor altar to be burned at a later time. They are extinguished now, so the wax has time to cool.)

((−)) Planes of Power:

> *"We release these elements of Hekate of Heaven, Earth and Sea, we are grateful for your lessons and their gifts, Blessings to all! So Mote it be! Hail and Farewell!"*

Opening the Circle:

Collection of offerings, passing out sign in contact sheet, and cakes and ale.

Hail and Farewell

At the end of the ritual all of the invocations or "calling in" must be released. This is to let the energies, spirits, and Goddess know the ritual is done for now, and they are appreciated and held in high regard. Most of the time we end with a *"Hail and farewell."* These are words of power to release any attachments and to move forward with the blessings and work done in ritual. They help to remove stagnation in the mind and body, allowing for your full potential to be revealed. The Goddess Hekate may come and go in your life, she wants you to walk with purpose, to be your own guide when you are able, and in times of uncertainty and doubt, she will come to your aide. This guidebook is simply a guide. As keeper of your life, you must use your own good judgement to accomplish the things that are your destiny. With the Titan Queen at your side, you are unconquerable.

Hail and Thank You.

Jennifer Teixeira is a High Priestess, Witch & Herbalist dedicated to Hekate, living deep in the Northern California Redwoods. She has contributed articles to Plant Healer Magazine and has contributed to the Starflower Covens Moon Newsletter. A woman of many witchy hats, Jennifer creates herbal products and offers magical items for sale at therootcutter.com.

Sources and further reading

The Aeneid, book VL, Virgil.

The Root Cutters, Sophocles

Giovan Battista Della Porta. From *De Miraculis Rerum Naturalium (The Wanderling)*, Book II, Chapter XXVI (1558 AD)

The Chaldean Oracles, G.R.S Mead

Circle for Hekate, Sorita D'Este

Hekate: A Devotional, Vivienne Moss

The Witching Herbs, Harold Roth

Keeping Her Keys, Cyndi Brannen

The Witch's Shield, Christopher Penczak

Pharmako/Poeia: Plant Powers, Poisons & Herbcraft, Dale Pendell

Road to Eleusis: Unveiling the Secrets of Eleusis, Gordon Wasson et al

For Puck's Sake - https://www.patheos.com/blogs matauryn/ 2017/07/19/many-epithets-hekate/

~"The Sacred Bee in Ancient Times and Folklore" by Hilda M. Ransome Chapter XI

~Apollonius Rhodius, Argonautica III 1036; cf. Ovid met VII. 24

**MOON
BOOKS**

PAGANISM & SHAMANISM

What is Paganism? A religion, a spirituality, an alternative belief system, nature worship? You can find support for all these definitions (and many more) in dictionaries, encyclopaedias, and text books of religion, but subscribe to any one and the truth will evade you. Above all Paganism is a creative pursuit, an encounter with reality, an exploration of meaning and an expression of the soul. Druids, Heathens, Wiccans and others, all contribute their insights and literary riches to the Pagan tradition. Moon Books invites you to begin or to deepen your own encounter, right here, right now.

If you have enjoyed this book, why not tell other readers by posting a review on your preferred book site.

Naming the Goddess
Trevor Greenfield
Naming the Goddess is written by over eighty adherents and
scholars of Goddess and Goddess Spirituality.
Paperback: 978-1-78279-476-9 ebook: 978-1-78279-475-2

Shapeshifting into Higher Consciousness
Heal and Transform Yourself and Our World with Ancient
Shamanic and Modern Methods
Llyn Roberts
Ancient and modern methods that you can use every day to
transform yourself and make a positive difference in the world.
Paperback: 978-1-84694-843-5 ebook: 978-1-84694-844-2

Readers of ebooks can buy or view any of these bestsellers by
clicking on the live link in the title. Most titles are published in
paperback and as an ebook. Paperbacks are available in traditional
bookshops. Both print and ebook formats are available online.

Find more titles and sign up to our readers' newsletter at
http://www.johnhuntpublishing.com/paganism
Follow us on Facebook at https://www.facebook.com/MoonBooks
and Twitter at https://twitter.com/MoonBooksJHP